A JOURNEY IN HEALING

From Longing To Sacred Unity

Linda A. Urbanski, Ph.D.

xulon
PRESS

A Journey in Healing
From Longing to Sacred Unity
by Linda A. Urbanski, Ph.D.

Printed in the United States of America

ISBN 978-1-60477-701-7

Unless otherwise indicated, Bible quotations are taken from The New American Bible. Copyright © 1970 by P.J. Kennedy & Sons.

www.xulonpress.com

DEDICATION

T his book is dedicated to the members and friends of Christian Center For Spiritual Healing and to all people who desire to live a spiritual life.

Table of Contents

Part II—Jesus' Experience: Strength For Our Journey
Jesus' Strength Becomes Our Strength

INTRODUCTION

The concept of a journey brings to mind not only the destination and travel required to arrive in the right place, at the right time, but also the process of preparing for the journey.

We can physically prepare by planning routes, packing bags, finalizing travel arrangements, and actually leaving the safety of our homes in order to embark on the journey. In addition to the physical preparation, spiritual and mental preparation is involved. Before we leave, we anticipate the sights to be seen, the people we will meet and the sounds that will touch our hearts and souls. Before we leave, we place our mail on hold, share contact information with others in the event of an emergency and squeeze a magazine or paperback into our carry-on bag. We do all that and more "just to be sure" that we have truly prepared for our trip.

Journeying is a process that takes time. It is on-going and active from the moment a trip is conceived in our mind, until we arrive home transformed by memories of people and places we have seen.

Journeying takes on a life of its own. It breathes with the energy of freedom, adventure and excitement. Journeying moves us from our current space to a new place where we can connect with the Divine on a deeper level and experience a sense of wholeness, harmony and oneness.

The Journey In Healing

This book presents healing from the perspective of a journey. In this manner, healing can be seen as an on-going process that involves grace, effort, time, thought, receptivity and growth, rather than an instantaneous cure. From this perspective, healing of the body, mind and/or spirit becomes part of the daily rhythm of our lives, leading toward a natural recognition and/or realization of our true essence in relation to God. God desires that we know all things are possible with and in Himself, regardless of the prognosis.

God manifests Himself for our benefit in many forms and offers grace through people, nature, beauty, love, writing, sports, music, technology and art. All of life becomes an opportunity to experience God and be transformed by His healing grace.

Similar to preparing for a journey out of state or out of the country, the journey in healing requires preparation. Preparation in this sense, involves taking time out from our busy lives to recognize moments of grace and to allow those moments to reside within our beings.

Dedicating time for ourselves is important. We need to respect our physical, emotional and mental limits. We need to stop to refresh and energize ourselves if only for a few moments each day. This act of making time for ourselves is an essential component of preparation that allows our bodies, minds and spirits to be open to receive healing energy in the form of grace.

The journey in healing also asks that we give ourselves time to allow the healing process to bring life, hope, joy, peacefulness, love, and a sense of harmony to our whole being. The healing journey asks that we befriend time and welcome all the wonder-filled, beauty-filled, grace-filled moments that accompany our desire for healing.

Promise Of Prayer Support

My prayers and the prayers of the members of Christian Center For Spiritual Healing will be with you as you enter more deeply into your journey of healing, into God's desire for you to experience wholeness. Please feel free to allow the healing process to unfold within you. You won't need to pre-plan or pre-program any aspect of this journey. Allow the healing process to guide you. Allow the healing process to impress your being and energize your intentions so that you will feel one with God.

All our intentions reside within the heart of God and are empowered by God. We simply need to remember that fact and live that realization.

We need to live our healing, live our oneness, live our wholeness and live our harmonization. We need to live our healing in a spirit of thankfulness, in a spirit of unconditional gratitude.

It has been my experience that journeys taken with others hold a special energy. The energy of the experience is magnified by the people who share the journey. It is my hope that in offering this format of supportive prayer, all of us who journey together will experience healing energy, not only for ourselves, but for all who rely on our prayers.

Suggestions

The format of this book is designed to facilitate a journey in healing. Each topic has been created and offered from the position that many of us will journey together as one people whose desire is to enter more deeply into the heart of God. As we grow more accustomed to the vibrations of the heart of God, we will recognize that Sacred Space as the place from which we came. We will find ourselves at home in God. We will desire to spend more time there and allow ourselves to be nurtured by His Grace for the sake of our healing and the healing of others.

The format is designed to provide you with messages from the heart of Jesus as shared through Scripture. Please refer to the entire passage to see the overall context of the setting and message. You'll find yourself better prepared to appreciate the fullness of the passage. Following the scripture passage is a reflection and an invitation to enter Sacred Space so as to be touched by the spirit of Jesus.

You are invited to use this book to actively *pray your journey in healing*. You may choose to highlight phrases that speak to your particular circumstance. Or, you may choose to pray with a notebook and record your thoughts, feelings, prayers and aspirations as they touch your spirit. Whatever method works best for you, allow the method to unfold as part of your daily prayer practice. Do not feel as if there is only one way to pray this journey.

Spend time with Jesus allowing the encounter to energize and empower your being. Expect to feel transformed by each encounter with Jesus because He truly desires to gift you with grace.

The Old Testament portrayed God as provider, forgiver, one who bestowed blessings in an outward way if certain conditions were met, or as One whose wrath could be expected if needed to protect His people. In some ways, this image of God conjured fear in the hearts and minds of many.

In the New Testament, Jesus referred to God as Father, but also in his experience, as an Ever-Living, Ever-Loving Presence, One who was so much more.

Jesus came to share his experience of oneness, harmony, and connection—living the statement "The Father and I are one." Jesus came to share his experience of God in order that people would love God from the depths of their being.

For our purpose, it is good to remember that during Jesus' time Mary, the mother of Jesus, was physically present to many of the people Jesus touched. She was able to affect their lives by her presence. She was able to be a channel of grace, a sign of receptivity for those she walked among. In effect, Jesus did not need to talk about the feminine attributes of a loving Mother, or a loving God. The personification of that aspect of God was already in their midst. The people only needed to look at Mary and the other women who followed Jesus to see God's love, compassion, and concern manifested in their midst.

Thoughts On Healing

Healing is living in God. Healing is living in the moment. Healing is living fully— in harmony, in peace, feeling connected to others, experiencing love, joy, courage, strength and compassion. Healing is journeying into God in oneness, with no separation.

Healing is living day to day in the space of God, in the place of our hearts where we recognize once and for all that we are one with God every moment of our lives. There is no separation. We are in the space of God totally loved and totally cared for. Healing is eternal wholeness, never-ending oneness, moving beyond ourselves into the gentle space that we come to recognize as the realm of Divine Unity. Healing is living in God always, everywhere, regardless of the circumstances.

Healing is living in God in connection with others, never alone, always as one family.

HEALING IS LIVING. HEALING IS LIVING IN GOD.

Part I—Journey In Healing

Chapter 1—Healing Is Living Fully

NEED

From the heart of Jesus: Matthew 6: 6, 8, 26-34

"Whenever you pray, go to your room, close your door and pray to your Father...
Your Father knows what you need before you ask him. Look at the birds in the sky. They do not sow or reap, they gather nothing into barns; yet your heavenly Father feeds them. Are you not more important than they? Which of you by worrying can add a moment to his life-span? As for clothes, why be concerned? Learn a lesson from the way the wild flowers grow. They do not work; they do not spin. Yet I assure you, not even Solomon in all his splendor was arrayed like one of these...Stop worrying, then, over questions like, 'What are we to eat, or what are we to drink, or what are we to wear? Your heavenly Father knows all that you need. Seek first his kingdom, his way of holiness, and all these things will be given you besides."

Reflection: Sometimes we grow overly concerned about our needs. They become so powerful that they take on an energy all of their own. Jesus reminds us that we don't need to be overwhelmed. We need not worry, grow anxious, nor become preoccupied, because in his experience of the Father, all is provided for. The Father knows all that we need. The Father is ever-present to us and our needs.

For Jesus, alignment/union with the Father is the response to all needs.

Situations in need of healing present us with opportunities to rely on this same attitude of Jesus, an attitude of aligning with the Father, an attitude of being united with the Father. The Father knows our needs and waits to respond with Life. We need to cultivate our consciousness to expect a response from the Father. We need not focus on what troubles us. We need to expect a response. By making space in our hearts and minds, grace does not have to fight for our attention. Grace is activated; it can be the divine solution to our needs. The Father's gift is grace, a divine solution to our needs. Let that divine solution enliven us and all those connected to us.

Invitation: In response to Jesus' words, you are invited to enter the sacred space within your being to align yourself with Jesus. It is a special place, a holy space where you feel comfortable, feel peaceful. Escort your need to that special place with the expectation that Jesus is already present waiting to welcome you. He is excited about this new level of confidence you have in his ability to meet your needs. Feel his excitement. Feel his desire to fill you with grace. Allow yourself to feel his grace fill your being for your benefit and the benefit of all in need. Feel Jesus flood you with his healing touch. Feel your heart respond to the heart of Jesus.

Bask in the warmth of his healing grace. There is no need to rush the experience. Remain in the space for as long as you desire. Give yourself time to allow Jesus' grace to transform your need. Feel the transformation occurring within your being.

Acknowledge the transformation and give thanks for the gift of new Life.

LIBERATION

From the heart of Jesus: Luke 9: 23-24

Jesus said to all: "Whoever wishes to be my follower must deny his very self, take up his cross each day, and follow in my steps. Whoever would save his life, will lose it, and whoever loses his life for my sake will save it."

Reflection: Jesus intuitively knew that to proceed to the next level of oneness, it would be necessary for the people of his day to look beyond their present situation. He knew they would need a human person to follow, an example, not some memory of a prophet, in order to see that oneness with God was truly possible.

Jesus challenged people to deny their very selves in order to see the future of possibilities and not be caught in the bonds of sickness, injustice, oppression and death. He encouraged them to embrace what most disturbed them in order to be in harmony with all that appeared outside of their reach, so that divine grace could further empower their beings.

Invitation: In response to Jesus' words you are invited to enter the sacred space within your being and meet Jesus in that space. You realize that the words he speaks can appear harsh—*deny self, take up your cross, follow*…You wonder if Jesus' words are really meant for you. You question if you can embrace them with your mind and heart. But you feel the peacefulness of Jesus' presence. You sense an aura of calm in his being. Jesus invites you to look with new eyes at your situation, to see the possibilities that present themselves to you. The cross that Jesus speaks of is not a cross of wood. It is a vehicle that leads to discovering your true self. Jesus invites you to embrace his desire to be totally present to his people and make that desire your own. Be totally present to yourself. Be totally present to others. Be totally present to each opportunity that raises your awareness of your place in God's plan for the benefit of others. Feel your heart respond in freedom to his invitation. Feel your need to move beyond your present situation. Jesus is present to lead you through this challenge. He knows by example that any experience that causes pain also contains the potential to liberate, to assist in transcending limitations. Jesus knows that and wants you to come to the same realization.

Jesus desires to liberate you from the bonds of fear, from all the second guessing of choices made along your journey. Jesus desires to free you from all that prevents you from being your True Self. Feel your heart respond to Jesus' invitation to embrace your True Self. Allow the grace of transformation/divine freedom to flood your being. Welcome that grace. Allow it to make its home in you. Feel refreshed, renewed.

Jesus is gifting you and all those connected to you with the grace of divine freedom. Acknowledge liberation from all that binds. Acknowledge unlimited possibilities, total mercy and forgiveness. Embrace divine freedom in this sacred moment and give thanks for the gift of new Life.

CELEBRATION

From the heart of Jesus: Matthew 9: 14-15

"Later on, John's disciples came to him with the objection, 'Why is it that while we and the Pharisees fast, your disciples do not?' Jesus said to them, *'How can the wedding guests go in mourning so long as the groom is with them?'"*

Reflection: Jesus answers a legitimate question with a question. His question tips the balance they are so familiar with from following every "prescription of The Law" and self-renunciation embraced by John the Baptist.

Jesus encourages John's disciples to be united with God by way of a celebration that brings life. He desires that they move beyond the thought that depriving themselves of nourishment is the only way to prepare for an encounter with God. Jesus desires to uplift their hearts and minds so that they can see through new eyes. Jesus refers to a common event, a wedding feast that speaks of the essence of God, the true nature of God—CELEBRATION!

Invitation: In response to Jesus' words, you are invited to enter the sacred space within yourself to align your spirit with the sentiments of Jesus. In that space allow yourself to reflect on all the times you have experienced God in life-giving events—wedding celebrations, births of children, grandchildren, nieces, nephews, baptisms, ordinations, anniversaries, graduations, song writing, celebrations of communal prayer, beautiful sunsets, late night walks on the beach, early morning bike rides, drinking from mountain springs, baseball, basketball and soccer games, dance recitals, healings from injuries or illnesses, planting trees and flowers, listening to favorite songs, celebrating lives of loved ones who have left this earth and now experience more fully the true essence of God, etc.

Allow these events to remind you of other events that were cause for celebration. Rekindle the wonder with Jesus. Feel his desire to relive all the special moments that have brought you closer to God and closer to the people you love. Allow your heart to be touched by the grace of celebrations of the past. Make space in your heart for the grace of celebrations yet to come.

Realize that this moment is a celebration — an opportunity to experience life in a new way, an opportunity to experience the blessings of God as Jesus did when he perceived each moment of life as filled with the Father's presence and never-ending love. Feel that love now. God desires that you experience Him as much as Jesus experienced Him. God wants you to celebrate his love for you and your love for others.

Give yourself time to feel God's love and *be love* for others. Feel the energy of celebration within your being as you experience love and embody love. Acknowledge the true power of celebration and give thanks for the gift of new life.

EXPECTATION

From the heart of Jesus: Luke 5: 27-29

Afterward he went out and saw a tax collector named Levi sitting at his customs post. He said to him, *"Follow me. Leaving everything behind, Levi stood up and became his follower."*

Reflection: Jesus' message was simple: follow me. Follow what I do. Live with me. Eat with me. Sing. Dance. Watch. Pray with me. Expect from the Father all that I expect. The blessings I receive are yours to receive. There's no magic involved, just a God who desires to be All, to be One With…in every situation.

Some, like Levi, truly heard Jesus' message. They heard not only with their ears, but with all their being and could do nothing else but follow. The words entered every cell of their bodies to transform their sense of expectation and desire for God to be God in their lives. The words would not allow them to stand still. The words demanded a response of trust.

Invitation: In response to Jesus' words allow yourself to return to the sacred space within. Listen closely. Quiet the noise. Dispel the distractions within and truly listen. Allow your heart to hear the message of healing, the message of forgiveness.

Whatever area is in need of healing, open that wounded space to hear Jesus' words, "Follow me…" Hear Jesus tell you to "leave everything behind"—leave behind the unpleasant memories, anger, embarrassment. Leave behind things spoken about you or against you. Leave behind the inability to believe, to have hope, to realize what your heart deeply desires. Leave behind all that drains you of life and embrace Jesus' words: "Follow me…" Allow your spirit to trust Jesus. Follow him as he walks toward a future of service, activity, relationships and vibrant health. Realize Jesus leads you. The same Jesus who experienced his own pain and the pain of others desires to move you through this moment. The same Jesus, who suffered because of who he was and the message he proclaimed, calls you to move beyond the limitations of this situation. He is confident that you will respond to his call.

Feel his grace stir within your mind and heart. Feel his grace walk through the pain-filled memories and liberate your entire being. The balm of healing love fills your whole self. Healing peace descends upon you. Remain in the moment with Jesus. Watch the flow of confidence from the heart of Jesus gently move into your heart. Jesus is healing you and there is no need to respond, simply accept his healing.

Expect Jesus' grace to transform you. Expect Jesus' grace to change the course of your life. Expect Jesus' grace to enliven you. Acknowledge the transformation and give thanks for the gift of life.

GOD IS HERE

From the heart of Jesus: Mark 1: 12-15

"...the Spirit sent him out toward the desert. He stayed in the wasteland forty days... After John's arrest, *Jesus appeared in Galilee proclaiming the good news of God: 'This is the time of fulfillment. The reign of God is at hand!'*"

Reflection: The most important message, the only message of Jesus has always been the same: the reign of God is right here, right now. There is no one, there is nothing else to wait for—God Is Here. God Is With Us— in every situation. It does not matter how we perceive the situation—good, bad, peaceful, conflicted, joyful or filled with chaos and confusion. God is here and waits for the realization of Jesus' message to come alive within us.

With God's presence present to us and for us, we are able to truly see all the possibilities available for us. No person, no situation can prevent us from experiencing oneness, union with God. Nothing can change the fact that this is kairos time for us. This is the time for Jesus to wake us up in the same way that Jesus went to Galilee to wake people up with this message. God Is Here. Jesus came to show the people, both then and now that God Is Here. God is present at this moment in time, and forever.

Invitation: In response to Jesus' words you are invited to enter the sacred space of the desert. In that space imagine Jesus welcoming you into the experience that he has shared for the last 40 days. He has known the unbearable heat of the day and the brisk chill of windy nights. He has known hunger, thirst, confusion within as he grappled with why he was there, why he felt compelled to share his experience of God. Allow Jesus to share his thoughts with you. Allow him to ignite the spark of enthusiasm within you so you too will know that *this* is your time to understand what he understood. Allow Jesus to kindle a fire in your heart, in your spirit to know beyond any doubt that God Is Present in all your situations. Dwell on the fact that *God is with you* in this encounter with Jesus. Sit in God's presence as if for the first time, and allow the flow of peacefulness, love, understanding and healing to fill your being.

Open your heart more fully to welcome God. Allow Jesus to introduce you to the God he so longed for and experienced more and more in his daily encounters with life, with people and in situations. Share all that is within your being. This is *your* desert-moment. This is *your* time of encounter. This is *your* time to be awakened to the mystery that *everything exists within God*. This is *your* time to know that God is present in all your situations for only one reason—to make you more aware of your divine connection and your connection to and for the benefit of others. You are invited to feel the excitement of knowing God is here for you and all of creation. Feel encouraged. Feel strengthened. Allow your whole being to accept this timeless blessing. God is here to empower you, your plans, your dreams, and your future with divine grace. Feel yourself being transformed by this realization and give thanks for the gift of the past, the present and the future. Give thanks for the gift of Presence.

DIVINE INHERITANCE

From the heart of Jesus: Matthew 25: 34-40

"...'Come. You have my Father's blessing! Inherit the kingdom prepared for you from the creation of the world. For I was hungry and you gave me food, I was thirsty and you gave me drink. I was a stranger and you welcomed me, naked and you clothed me. I was ill and you comforted me, in prison and you came to visit me...'"

Reflection: Jesus tells the people in no uncertain terms: You have my Father's blessing. You don't need to do any thing special, just be your true selves. Act from your heart. Respond to people in need. Enter into their experience, not so much to dwell on the experience, or feel sorry for them, but to lift them out of it. Feed, clothe, welcome, visit... Bless others by your actions. Act from the space of divine inheritance. Act as if all is available for your use to sustain others. Every blessing is already yours and has been for all time. There is no law governing blessings.

Jesus already knew that for the Father to be Father, the Father needs to give, to bestow, to bless. For the Father to be Father, he needs to offer all that is himself—everything to everyone without exception, without limitation, without hesitation. Jesus knew this about the Father. Jesus knew the Father did not place conditions on his people. Jesus knew the Father loved and blessed unconditionally. Jesus needed people to see the Father through his eyes. Jesus tells them the time of liberation is now. Inherit what is yours from the beginning: potential, abundance, liberation. Inherit what is yours and has been for all time.

Invitation: In response to Jesus' words allow yourself to enter the sacred space of need. Close your eyes. Open your heart and sit with Jesus. Watch the people who come to him in need of health, food, shelter, work, love, companionship, oneness, etc. Women, men and children are coming to Jesus—some come with hope, others have no hope left within them. Listen to their words of concern, of pain. Reach out to them in their need. Embrace them. Be a sign of grace for them with Jesus.

You are overwhelmed by all that is lacking. You notice Jesus is not frazzled or flustered. He simply moves among them with a word, a gesture, a smile. You take it all in and wonder how he can remain so peaceful, so confident.

The crowd diminishes and you are alone again with Jesus. He senses your confusion.

He asks how he can help you or those you love. He encourages you to share what consumes your being. He desires to open your eyes and heart to the reality of divine inheritance. He asks what causes your insecurity. He invites you to name the place of insecurity and allow it to become your *Altar of Transformation*. He tells you not be afraid, for needs are but one path to the realization of divine inheritance. You hear yourself reciting a litany of needs for family, friends and self. Jesus smiles and tells you to bless each need. You bless and watch as each person, situation becomes transformed. You bless and realize how greatly you have been blessed by the experience. Give thanks for the gift of blessing and the responsibility to bless.

IDENTIFICATION

From the heart of Jesus: Matthew 6:7-15

"... 'Your Father knows what you need before you ask him. This is how you are to pray: Our Father in heaven, hallowed be your name, your kingdom come...' "

Reflection: More than once Jesus indicates to the people of his time that the Father knows what everyone needs. This repetition is not a coincidence. It is reinforcement. Jesus repeats the theme that all we need is already known by the Father. We simply must identify with that knowledge. We must embrace the concept that we know the Father knows all about our needs and wants to provide for those needs. We need to surrender to that knowledge to experience the Oneness Jesus knew. We need to accept our needs as a way to grow in *dependence* upon the Father.

In our hearts, in our minds we need to believe that our needs are merely a reminder to remember the Father is capable of providing for all. The Father is All. We know that in our heart of hearts. We need to elevate our concerns to that level of Oneness, that level of fulfillment known intimately by Jesus. We need not be afraid to experience the Father at that level. We need not be afraid to be *dependent* in the same way Jesus was dependent on the Father.

Invitation: In response to Jesus' words, you are invited to enter the sacred space of your being and meet with Jesus. Allow your mind and heart to feel a sense of peace, a sense of freedom knowing God is aware of your needs and the needs of all people, in all time, in every place. Feel a sense of confidence that your needs are not separate from everyone else's needs, but part of the composition of who we are as One Family. Feel a sense of liberation in that knowledge. Feel a sense of responsibility to care for those whose needs are greater than your own.

Allow yourself to sit as if in front of a divine fountain of grace. With Jesus, be the one in need, as well as the one who responds to needs. There is no difference. The one in need is the same as the responder to the need. In that sacred space, accept all in confidence, accept all knowing that a blessing has already been given and needs only to be acknowledged. Accept all needs for those unable to accept their needs. Surround the needs with divine grace. In that sacred space, the wonder of God is manifested. The divine fountain of grace cannot run dry. Return to the fountain. Expect to be showered with blessings.

Goodness, mercy, genuine concern will always be the response of God as delivered first by Jesus and now, by you and all God's people. Identify with Jesus. Identify with his response. With Jesus, see all in harmony—people, situations, disease processes, warring factions, all of creation. See with the eyes of Jesus, feel with the heart of Jesus, touch with the hands of Jesus. Watch in wonder as the transformations take place. Your heart now knows God needs us to identify with his desire to respond to all situations so that all in need will experience the depth of divine love. Respond in order to bring about the realization of the Kingdom within the hearts of all in need. Touch, extend a blessing of wholeness, of peace, of healing. Speak the words—"know you are loved, know you are cared for." Give thanks for the gift of realization.

VALIDATION

From the heart of Jesus: Luke 11: 29-32

"While the crowds pressed around him he began to speak these words: 'This generation seeks a sign, but no sign will be given it except the sign of Jonah. Just as Jonah was a sign for the Ninevites, *so the Son of Man will be a sign for the present age'*."

Reflection: Jesus knew that each generation needs and looks for signs—a validation, an affirmation that what they are looking for is already present to them. Their deepest needs, desires, can and will be fulfilled in one they can see, touch, and mingle with— the Son of Man in their midst.

Jesus' message is simple—it is available to and for all—There is no limitation. What the Father bestows on the Son, the Father will bestow on all sons and daughters. The Father desires oneness, unity with all his children. The Father desires to offer healing energy to all in need. The Father sends Jesus as a sign of his ever-presence, his perpetual willingness to offer himself to his children.

Invitation: In response to Jesus' words, you are invited to enter the sacred space within your being and ask yourself if you need a sign, if you need validation that God is present in your situation or the situations of your friends/loved ones. If you find yourself saying, "yes" find peace in that feeling. Find comfort in your ability to trust God enough to ask for a sign. Requesting validation is not a form of weakness or lack of faith. Asking for validation is a sign of our belief that God truly cares to communicate His love, His concern for us and our situations. God comes to meet us where we are—in our questioning, confusion and inability to see beyond the situation. God inserts Himself into those difficult moments. God is present in the messy, the pain-filled, and the devastating situations we find ourselves in. God is comfortable with our mess. He does not expect us to reach out to Him on any special terms or only when we feel alive, vibrant and ready to sing His praise.

In the sacred space, Jesus invites you to share your need for a sign. He encourages you to remove the barrier of "spiritual correctness" and pour out your heart to Him. Jesus knows that God responds to that level of intense prayer for he too, often prayed from the depths of his heart when he was in need. Allow Jesus to hold you in the sacred space. His sign of love, of caring is God present in your situation. Jesus' desire to know all about what causes such deep pain is in reality, God's desire to be one with you in your need. God clings to you through Jesus in this moment. This is your moment of validation. This is your moment when God desires to move the pain out of your being in order to replace the pain with hope. Allow God's love and compassion to act like a wave. Feel it slowly move through your being. The wave is gentle. It collects your fear, your sense of helplessness and feelings of hopelessness. The wave carries that energy away from your mind, spirit and heart. It releases the energy into the divine space to be sanctified, to be made pure. What caused so much concern now returns to you in divine form. The wave breaks and washes over you bringing a sense of hope, calm, peace and healing. Relax in the wave and give thanks for validation.

ABUNDANCE

From the heart of Jesus: Matthew 7:7-12

"Ask, and you shall receive. Seek and you shall find. Knock, and it will be opened to you. For the one who asks, receives; the one who seeks, finds. The one who knocks, enters. If you know how to give your children what is good, how much more will your heavenly Father give good things to anyone who asks him."

Reflection: Jesus was able to alter his message for each group he spoke to. To this group, he felt action was required on their part. As a result, he encouraged them to ask and indicated if they asked, they would receive. Jesus didn't say maybe they would receive. He didn't say if it was good for them, they would receive. He said, ask and you will receive, implying that no request was out of bounds, implying no request would go unanswered.

Jesus' experience was that God's love and depth of concern for His people is limitless. God could transform any request into an answer, a positive solution.

Jesus' experience was that God desires to be asked. God waits to be asked. God waits to be invited to respond to situations most in need. Imagine—a God who waits for us...how unfamiliar, how awesome! A God who waits...

Invitation: You are invited to move into your sacred space and experience the growing crowds that caused Jesus to move up the mountainside when he spoke with them. Find a spot near Jesus and breathe in the energy of nature, of people's needs and the simplicity of Jesus' message. Take it all in. Truly allow yourself to be open to the moment. Find yourself hearing the words "Ask, you shall receive" in a new way.

Seek, knock...you've heard these words so many times, but allow them to sink deeper into your being. Feel Jesus' excitement as he relays this simple message to people so accustomed to following the prescriptions of the Law in order to be blessed by God. See yourself asking for resolution to your concern or the concerns of those close to you. See each situation change as a result of the gift of God's breath, God's grace. Watch health, harmony and confidence replace sickness, conflict and insecurity. Realize all situations can be transformed in this moment. Realize transformation is possible if only you would use your words to ask.

God waits for the power of your words. God uses your breath to create something new, something unimaginable within your situation. God uses your words, your breath to call forth life, to manifest abundance. God waits and allows you to help create the present, to inspire the future you so deeply desire with and in Him. God waits to meet us where we are in order to lead us to a new place of knowing Him more deeply. Breathe in Jesus. Breathe in God. Allow the breath to refresh and renew you and all those close to you. Wait with God. Wait in God. Feel the energy of His abundant love and mercy fill your being. Offer love and mercy to all people in need. Let God's love and mercy flow through you through your breath. Bless all creation with divine abundance. Bless the sky, the mountains, the waters, the entire human family with the power of words. Bless all situations and feel the blessings of others descend upon you. Give thanks for the divine gift of abundance.

HARMONY

From the heart of Jesus: Matthew 5: 20-26

"If you bring your gift to the altar and there recall that your brother has anything against you, go first to be reconciled with your brother, and then come and offer your gift."

Reflection: Jesus shared a secret with those who listened to his words. Harmony with individuals, reconciliation with those who have hurt us or we have hurt, is required before bringing any gift or petition to God. Harmony within our beings, and in our relationships with others, is essential to for us to feel the power of God.

God works within us. God offers grace for every situation. However, to feel the impact of that grace and energy, we need to let go of all that poisons us, all the negativity that occupies the space where healing energy could reside within our being. We need to release what consumes us in order to be free to experience harmony and oneness.

Invitation: You are invited to return to your sacred space and cover your head and heart with a cloak of compassion. Draw the cloak over your being and ask that Jesus lead you to the Altar of Woundedness. At the altar you can release the words, the actions, the omissions, the betrayals that have caused you the most pain. In the presence of Jesus, bring the situations to the altar. Place them on the altar with a blessing. Offer them in peace, in freedom. Feel your heart become liberated from their wounding grasp. Allow the pressure, the tension in your mind to release its hold on your being. The words, the actions, the betrayals, the omissions do not have power over you any longer. You have opened yourself to the grace of compassion. Mercy fills your being. Feel mercy, feel forgiveness flow through you making you whole. Remain wrapped in the cloak of compassion until you feel whole.

At the same Altar of Woundedness, Jesus invites you to draw from the wellspring of mercy and to reconcile with those you have hurt by your words or actions. In this sacred space all are one. You can forgive and ask forgiveness. You can make whole while being made whole. Offer the cloak of compassion to any one in need, any one you have wounded. Place the cloak over their head and heart and bless them by your expression of sorrow. Step back and allow them freedom, space and time to accept God's gift of mercy. Step back as they recognize that compassion can fill their beings with more power than indifference and hatred. Watch as Jesus moves closer to the Altar. A fountain on the Altar of Woundedness now flows with unending mercy. Crowds of people gather to be released of pain and filled with divine compassion and harmony. They move around the altar slowly as if in a dance. The wounded and the ones who inflicted the wounds merge into one family. Mercy magnifies. Compassion abounds. The Altar expands to accommodate more people. How great the realization that many wounded are now healed. Many now desire to share mercy with others. Acknowledge the blessings of this experience and give thanks for the ability to live in harmony with all people.

TRUE SELF

From the heart of Jesus: Matthew 5: 43-48

"My command to you is: love your enemies, pray for your persecutors. This will prove that you are children of your Heavenly Father, for his sun rises on the bad and the good, he rains on the just and the unjust. If you love those that love you, what good is there in that? *...you must be made perfect as your heavenly Father is perfect.*"

Reflection: Jesus' experience of the Father is one of total union. In his experience, there is no separation, no sense of want, abandonment, rejection. His portrayal of the Father as perfect, and challenge to others to embrace perfection is simply Jesus being Jesus. He wants the experience that he has felt and known with the Father to be our experience. He desires that we become that same experience of perfection for others so they will know oneness, harmony, abundance, and acceptance.

Jesus' challenge was not idealistic. It simply was a call to people to be who they truly are—images of God, images of unlimited possibilities. Jesus' call to elevate thoughts and actions was and still remains a call to identify and live from the higher Self, the Divine present within and within all relationships.

Invitation: In response to Jesus' words allow yourself to enter your sacred space. With an open heart and mind, desire to see yourself acting from a state of perfection in all your dealings with people. Begin with the people you love. Draw out the best from them. Compliment them, build their confidence and tell them how deeply you value their gift of presence. Watch their faces glow with wonder. Watch their eyes brighten with surprise. Remain in that space with the ones you love. Invite them to invite people they love. Watch as the group grows and the energy of divine perfection expands. Hold the space with your heart. This is a special moment, a moment that empowers all involved.

In the presence of Jesus, invite those who stir conflict within you to enter this same space. Although the mood changes and people seem unsure, greet them with sincerity, comfort and compassion. In your heart see them through the eyes of God. See them as already perfect. See them as their True Selves, vessels of divine grace living their own mystery. Bless their mystery. Bless their place as sons and daughters, in the family of God. Realize their True Self is their only Self waiting to emerge from behind the mask of fear, the mask of insecurity. Invite the True Selves to join in the sacred gathering. Expect the best from them. Encourage them. Expect that they too desire to operate from their True Selves. Perhaps no one ever saw the True Self in them. Perhaps no one ever greeted them with mercy and compassion. With Jesus, create an environment of acceptance. With Jesus, make this moment their sacred moment—their moment of realization that they too are sons and daughters in the Divine Family. Divine love and caring fill the room. Separation and conflict give way to oneness and harmony. All are images of God in this moment. All act from their Highest Self and desire to invite others to live from their True Self. The group expands once again. Mercy is limitless. Compassion knows no bounds. Perfection is the norm. Acknowledge oneness and peace in the sacred space and give thanks.

DO SOMETHING

From the heart of Jesus: Matthew 9: 2-9

"…people brought to him a paralyzed man lying on a mat. When Jesus saw their faith he said to the paralytic,'Stand up! Roll *up your mat, and go home!'* The man stood up and went toward his home. At the sight a feeling of awe came over the crowd, and they praised God…"

Reflection: Jesus knew people needed outward signs to move them from their current way of thinking into a new mindset where they could experience unlimited potential. He knew he could have forgiven the paralytic's sin, as was the custom for one afflicted, but chose another route. Within earshot of the crowd, Jesus told the paralytic to stand up. He told him to move from a position of dependence into a position of readiness. He told him, take action—roll up your mat. He told him, do something—don't just stand there in amazement. He told him, go home—show your family, your friends the endless possibilities that also await them. Not only did he free the paralytic from his mat, he liberated the hearts of all in the crowd. He helped them move from fear of God into praise of God. He touched all their hearts with his directive to *"Stand up!"* He triggered action within their beings by encouraging them to "roll up" all the ideas that kept them bound and told them to "return home" to their True Selves to be a blessing for others.

Invitation: You are invited to return to your Sacred Space and prepare yourself to meet Jesus. He wants to share his excitement of the encounter with the crowd who brought him the paralytic. You listen as he speaks to your heart. As he recounts the story, you hear the words "Stand up" as if spoken to you. You open your heart and allow all the emotions that have kept your spirit down to move outside your being. You feel lighter. Memories no longer weigh you down. You hear Jesus encourage you to "roll up" every experience that caused you pain. You find yourself "rolling the experiences up in a quilt" near your feet. You begin to embrace the quilt. In the Sacred Space with Jesus you find the grace to lift up the quilt and present it to him. In that moment of elevation, you sense a change within yourself. Jesus draws the quilt to his heart and kisses it. In watching Jesus tenderly embrace all that hurt you, you experience a new found freedom. The experiences that once caused so much pain have now been blessed by Jesus. They no longer seem so ominous. They no longer hold the power to wound you. You find yourself at peace with the people and situations associated with the experiences. You bless them as Jesus blessed them. You set them free to be at peace in the Sacred Space of Jesus.

In the eyes of Jesus you see a sense of satisfaction. You blessed, as he blessed. You embraced, as he embraced. Your heart led you to the One Heart from which only grace and blessings flow. In thanksgiving for the experience take your quilt and bless all who have been wounded. Bless the sick, the hungry, the thirsty, the lonely, the forgotten. Bless the people of war-torn lands. Bless the sky, seas and earth. Bless those without hope and those who bring hope. Give thanks for being able to bless. Give praise. Sing praise.

RETURN TO YOUR ROOTS

From the heart of Jesus: Luke 2: 41-51a

"His parents used to go every year to Jerusalem for the feast of Passover and when he was twelve they went up for the celebration as was their custom. As they were returning at the end of the feast, the child Jesus remained behind unknown to his parents. …Not finding him, they returned to Jerusalem in search of him. When his parents found him, his mother said to him: 'Son, why have you done this to us? You see that your father and I have been searching for you in sorrow.' He said to them:

'Why did you search for me? *Did you not know I had to be in my Father's house?'*"

Reflection: As an innocent child, Jesus speaks from his heart to parents who he felt should have understood, should have known better. Jesus felt that they should have known where to find him when they noticed that he was missing. Jesus felt that they should have known he would gravitate toward the place and space where he could move deeper into God.

In the confusion of the festivities, Jesus returned to his roots, to that which was most familiar to him. In our own confusion, we too are invited to go to the space, to the place where God is most familiar, most present to us—the place where we can touch the healing energy of Jesus— the place where the energy of abundance and new opportunities await us.

Invitation: You are invited to return to your Sacred Space. In that space surround yourself with an image of a celebration that has been significant to you. Allow the memories of that celebration to rekindle a sense of excitement within your being. Allow them to spark hope in areas that need to be transformed. This celebration holds the power to transform. This celebration did not end when the last guest left. It remains within your heart and mind to energize you whenever you are in need.

Jesus is seated in your Sacred Space enjoying your recollection of a celebration. He is reminded of his return to the Temple as a twelve year old. He remembers how he "had to be" in his Father's house. He remembers how at peace, how comfortable he was in that setting. He invites you now to bask in the energy of your memories. He invites you to allow those memories to nourish your being and lift you up.

Jesus invites you to remember how the music of the celebration filled you with life and hope. He invites you to remember how the conversations filled you with love and caring. He invites you to remember how the laughter of the little children filled you with joy and pride. The grace of this memory-filled experience returns you to your roots. It takes you back to a time when all was in harmony within your being, within your relationships. You know that same sense of harmony, of well-being is possible once again because of Jesus. He has helped you to experience the grace of happiness, peace, joy and health in this moment. You now realize Jesus will lead you into the future with that same desire for wholeness. Give thanks for all the celebrations that have touched your life. Give thanks for all the celebrations that have yet to come.

Bless the memories, the roots of God.

OPEN TO SERVE

From the heart of Jesus: Matthew 23: 1-12

"...The greatest among you will be the one who serves the rest."

Reflection: Jesus begins to tip the scales. Old formulas, once so important, no longer matter. The hierarchy is being reestablished. The one who is accustomed to being served is now being called upon to serve. The thought can not be understood by some. The act of service becomes revolting to others who have always been served.

Jesus' life indicates that service to another has astounding potentiality. It will truly open one's eyes and heart like never before. Service is the position of receptivity we all are called to. It is the position of God who waits to be called on—waits to be invited into the special circumstances where there is need. Service of the entire family of God is a privilege. Service is assuming the role of God.

Invitation: You are invited to enter your Sacred Space to meet Jesus, the Servant. It is in this space that Jesus desires to gift you with Servant-Grace, the grace of one who totally abandons his/hers dreams and aspirations and empties him/herself of all desires and ideas in order to be a vessel of love and compassion for the benefit of others. The Sacred Space of the Servant is a vulnerable place. It is a holy place. It is a place of chaos. Your heart and soul will be broken as you are filled with Servant-Grace. Trust Jesus in this moment. Trust Jesus to lead you through this experience.

Give your heart and soul to Jesus without conditions. Allow Jesus to prepare you to live from your True Self, the Servant Self.

Servant-Grace fills the air in this Sacred Space. You are invited to inhale it and allow it to renew and refresh every cell of your being. Allow it to transform your memories. Allow it to recreate your heart and make it more open to the needs of others. Servant-Grace allows you to anticipate the needs of others. It will gift you with words others need to hear. Servant-Grace will move through your being and empower you with the tendencies and tenderness of Jesus.

Jesus invites you to respond to areas of need with Servant-Grace. He invites you in this moment to embrace family/business situations, medical conditions, people in need and offer the gift of divine grace for the situation. You are their servant. You are present to meet their needs in the space of Jesus. People continue to come to you and Jesus. You touch, you share a word and you heal. With Servant-Grace, you meet them in their need and transform their need by a response. The people continue to come. As grace fills the room, people in need begin to respond to others in need. Everyone begins to anticipate the needs of others. They are practicing Servant-Grace. Compassion permeates the Sacred Space. Compassion is Servant-Grace in another form. You acknowledge the gift of compassion and give thanks for the experience of being a servant.

CONNECTION

From the heart of Jesus: Matthew 20:17-28

"Anyone among you who aspires to greatness must serve the rest and whoever wants to rank first among you must serve the needs of all. Such is the case with the Son of Man who has come, not to be served by others, but to serve, to give his own life for the many."

Reflection: For two consecutive days the Book of Matthew offers Jesus' understanding of what it means to be great. To be great means to serve others — to be open, to be attentive and responsive to the needs of others.

Service is power. Service is connection to and with others. Service is the concrete manifestation of God. Service is God present among God's people, as one deeply concerned for the well-being, the wholeness of all people.

Jesus was familiar with service. Service was a way of life for him. Jesus was attentive to the physical, mental, and spiritual needs of the people who followed him. Service was the catalyst that called forth compassion from within his heart. Service challenges us to live as Jesus lived, poured out for others.

Invitation: You are invited to enter your Sacred Space. In that space allow yourself to be open to experience connection with the Servant, Jesus. Jesus waits there for you. He eagerly seeks to share a new level of connection with you.

As you move into the Sacred Space you feel Jesus. You feel his desire to speak without words. He leads you to Mary, his mother, the one who taught him to serve. He invites you to watch as she serves. Like many mothers, Mary saw the needs of her family and responded to those needs. Like many mothers, Mary emptied herself in order to give to others. You are reminded of your own mother and the examples she set for you. She always placed others first. She gave life and continues to be a life-giving force for her family and friends. She fed the hungry. She cared for sick relatives and friends. She worked to make life easier for the family. Early in the morning she spoke of the sun, wind and heat in order to anticipate what the day would bring. In the evening she gently calmed fears to prepare for a night of rest.

Jesus draws your attention to service by example, service by connection. He offers you the opportunity to be of service to others. As you agree to serve and connect, you find yourself surrounded by a field of wild flowers. The flowers beckon to you. They too desire to serve. You gently pick an armful of flowers and begin to distribute them. You move toward the mother whose children have been scared and scarred by violence. She accepts the flowers and presses them to her heart. You enter the home of a middle-aged man suffering from cancer. His family surrounds his bedside. He is so afraid to die. You give him a wildflower. He breathes in its sweet fragrance and for a moment feels so alive. You share flowers with the family. In that moment death disappears. Thoughts of life, only life abound. You begin to understand service, connection. It is so natural. It is so Jesus-like. Give thanks and bless that realization.

Chapter 4—Healing Is Living In The Moment

CONSOLATION

From the heart of Jesus: Luke 16: 19-31

"Once there was a beggar named Lazarus who was covered with sores. Lazarus longed to eat the scraps that fell from the rich man's table. The dogs even came and licked his sores. Eventually, the beggar died. He was carried by the angels to the bosom of Abraham. The rich man likewise died and was buried. From the abode of the dead where the rich man was in torment, he raised his eyes and saw Abraham afar off, and Lazarus resting in his bosom. He called out, 'Father Abraham, have pity on me'… 'My child, replied Abraham, 'remember that you were well off in your lifetime, while Lazarus was in misery. Now *he has found consolation here.'…"*

Reflection: Everyone is in search of solace, of being understood in a way that brings wholeness. At some point in life, we all need to have our hearts held in the gentle hands of another to gain strength, feel loved, and be energized by that love.

We seek consolation through our brokenness and find healing and liberation through relationships. We seek consolation in places where we encounter the grace and energy of Jesus. Grace may fill us directly from the heart of Jesus. Grace may flow from Scripture, or through the words of another trying to impart Jesus' healing energy by following Jesus' actions. Grace may express itself in the energy of love directed to us by the ones who love us most. All are forms of consolation. All are available to us. It is up to us to be receptive.

Invitation: You are invited to enter your Sacred Space and be filled with the grace of consolation. Jesus is present. He shares the story of the rich man and Lazarus with you. You understand, yet begin to question an aspect of the story. Lazarus was comforted. Lazarus found consolation after a life of want, a life of need. You look at Jesus and tell him you understand how Lazarus would be ministered to, but you begin to question why in death, the rich man was not ministered to. You think compassion, consolation should have been offered to the rich man as well, in spite of how he treated others during his life. You wonder what traumatized his life so deeply that he was unable to move beyond himself to help another. You wonder why, how he could live so self-centered. Jesus begins to smile. Jesus knows that in this realization you now know true compassion, true consolation.

Jesus invites you to surround all people with compassion. Jesus encourages you to offer consolation to all regardless of their situations, their shortcomings, their lack of response to others' needs. You stop and breathe deeply. You fill your heart until you realize that compassion and consolation are now flowing out of your being for the benefit of others. With Jesus, your heart acts as a vessel of grace. You offer acceptance and understanding to all in need and above all, to those who do not even realize they are in need of grace. With Jesus you offer light, goodness, concern to those who have lost their way. You reach out with Jesus and welcome all in need of wholeness, of healing. You acknowledge consolation, compassion, generosity of spirit and give thanks for the gift of every person's life. You give thanks for Life.

OPENINGS

From the heart of Jesus: Matthew 21: 33-43, 45-46

"The stone which the builders rejected has become the keystone of the structure. It was the Lord who did this and we find it marvelous to behold."

Reflection: Jesus' message at times was veiled in images to emphasize the point he was trying to convey. The images formed a tangible picture in people's hearts and minds taking on a life of their own to grow within them and transform belief systems held so dear.

In this instance, Jesus refers to himself as the stone the builders rejected. His very life, his way of living is the outward manifestation of the message he tries to convey. His message can be accepted by some, but also rejected by many. Yet even in rejection, the messenger continues to bring life. Jesus leads us to see that the ideas we ignore, the people we reject and the situations that confuse us represent the door by which grace will enter.

Invitation: You are invited to enter your Sacred Space. The focal point of the space is a fire tended by Jesus. He uses a stick to move the wood in order for air to circulate among the pieces and increase the flames. You are drawn to the warmth of the fire and hear it crackle as if trying to share a message with you. You are mesmerized by the beauty of the flames. As the flames rise you feel as if part of yourself is being caught up in their mystery. You move closer as if part of their dance.

Jesus invites you to surrender all that is blocked within you to the mystery of the flames. The flames will become your opening. The flames contain all that you are searching for—excitement, passion, commitment to something greater than yourself. The flames depict ultimate surrender as they give of themselves in order to provide light and warmth. The flames invite you to be yourself as they are themselves. They burn because they are fire. You love because you are a manifestation of God.

You surrender all that you thought you had to be. You give up memories, words that have caused confusion. You simply present yourself before the flames and ask Jesus to stir joy, rekindle hope and strengthen the divine connection within you. Jesus knows what you are asking for. He remembers his desert venture when he begged the Father for the same. He knows how all the challenging experiences can be used as openings for grace. He knows rejection can be used as a catalyst to draw some to believe and live the dream of one divine family committed to the service of all. Jesus knows you know that too. Jesus knows you are one who can commit to loving and caring for all people. He asks you to join in his mission.

The flames purify you of all that restrains you. The smoke rises taking your deepest intentions to the heart of God. In that moment you see an opening. You are at peace.

You are filled with vitality. You feel connected to those you love and serve. With Jesus you see many more openings and give thanks for Life.

VESSEL OF GRACE

From the heart of Jesus: Luke 1: 26-38

"Upon arriving, the angel said to her: Rejoice, O highly favored daughter! The Lord is with you. Blessed are you among women. She was deeply troubled by his words, and wondered what the greeting meant. The angel went on to say to her: 'Do not fear, Mary. You have found favor with God.' ..."

Reflection: The beginning of the story of Jesus is really Mary's response to the fear she initially felt when greeted by the angel. Hesitantly she embraced the angel's message. She would be part of a bigger plan. She would allow her life to be used to affect the lives of others.

A vessel to carry grace, to energize yet another sign of God present among His people — that was Mary's role; a woman-channel of God who desired to gift people with one who could lead them to believe in another way. The God of Abraham was all people believed God to be — the God of fire, clouds and Manna in the desert, the God of blessings in response to adherence to The Law, the God of sacrifice, the God of protection from tribes who wanted their land, etc. Yet God was so much more. The potential available to all people would be limitless. God would live among His people in the person of Jesus, Mary's son. Grace would be available for all times.

Invitation: You are invited to enter your Sacred Space. A vessel stands in the corner of the room. Jesus sits next to the vessel. He encourages you to sit by his side. You focus your eyes on the vessel. You admire its beauty and at the same time, it's fragility. You realize that this vessel will break even if it is only gently disturbed. Jesus senses your concern for the vessel. You hear him say that this vessel is meant to be broken. The contents of this vessel are meant to be poured out for all in need. You seem a bit dismayed. You wonder how something so precious, so uniquely adorned, could have been made to be broken in order for it to be itself, to be of service. The thought finds resonance within.

A crowd begins to fill the room. They make their way toward you and Jesus. Jesus invites you to break the vessel. He encourages you to dip your hand in the oil contained within. He desires that you experience this oil of blessing. You feel overwhelmed by the grace of this moment. Jesus asks you to draw out more oil and share its blessings with the crowd. Jesus also takes some of the oil and moves toward those unable to come to him. The oil flows freely. People are open to receive the oil.

People continue to fill the sacred space. They desire to be blessed and also to bless.

Jesus distributes the oil to them so that they too can share this blessing with friends and family. They receive from the vessel of blessing and in turn become a blessing for others. The room slowly empties. Only you and Jesus remain. Jesus invites you to hold the experience in your heart. He invites you to return to your heart, your personal vessel of grace, each time you find someone in need. You appreciate Jesus entrusting you with this gift of blessing. You bow your head and give thanks for the gift of Life.

FOUNTAIN OF LIFE

From the heart of Jesus: John 4: 5-42

"...whoever drinks the water I give him, will never be thirsty; no the water I give shall become a fountain within him, leaping up to provide eternal life..."

Reflection: Seated at the well, Jesus once again defies the custom of his tradition by speaking to the Samaritan woman who comes to draw water. Intuitively, he knows she is ready for this moment because as he speaks to her, she shows no fear. He asks her for a drink and invites her into his space. Alone, by the well, Jesus can be himself. He can offer his message to her without the people of his day questioning why he is speaking to a woman.

The message he shares is that all people are entitled to experience union, oneness with God — in this case, even a Samaritan woman. He shares the fact that there is no reason for want or hunger, no reason for thirst. A fountain of life, of grace, of energy lives within all. The fountain of life is Divine Grace flowing freely for all.

Invitation: You are invited to enter your Sacred Space. The mood in the space is festive, joyful. The vibrations lift up your heart and mind. You sense something exciting is about to happen. You anticipate the encounter will be very powerful.

In the center of the room, Jesus is seated at a well. He indicates that he is thirsty and seeks to be refreshed. People respond to Jesus' thirst by offering him something to drink. Jesus is refreshed. Jesus feels renewed. Jesus allows himself to be dependent upon the goodness and generosity of others. He allows them to reach into the fountain of life within themselves in order to tap into Divine Grace.

As Jesus' thirst is quenched, he looks at you. He invites you to drink from the fountain of life. He invites you to fill yourself with Divine Grace. You do not hesitate. You gladly receive this gift. You find your thirst quenched, your hunger satisfied. In your heart friends and family appear before you. You know their needs.

You know their hunger, their desire for health, for wholeness, for relationship. You accompany them to the well to be renewed and refreshed by Divine Grace. You watch attentively while others minister to their needs. You watch as they grow stronger with each cup of blessing offered to them.

The water rises from the well and washes over the entire world. It blesses all the places where blood has been spilt by war and destruction. It bathes areas suffering from drought or destroyed by fires. It purifies land scarred by nuclear accidents and human indifference. The waters of eternal grace wash over the world in a gentle manner. There is no fear of a divine tsunami. Grace purifies and dedicates the entire world for one purpose—renewal of hope, joy and love. The Fountain of Life flows for all without exception. Conditions do not exist. Limitations disappear. Grace is abundant. Allow the energy of this moment to wash over you and give thanks for the gift of new Life.

COMFORT LEVELS

From the heart of Jesus: Luke 4: 24-30

"He went straight through their midst and walked away."

Reflection: The same message of Jesus that touched people's hearts upset others to the point that they wanted the messenger stopped. They did not want to lose their positions of power, their ability to oppress, nor their belief systems. They would fight to defend their comfort levels. They would hold on to what they held most dear.

Jesus was not one to force his message upon any one. If people were ready to embrace his way of living, he would continue to share the message with them. However, if they weren't ready for the message he would walk away. Jesus did not force his message upon any one. He would leave people in the midst of their conflict so as not to create additional confusion within. Jesus would allow people to be themselves until they returned to him searching for more.

Invitation: You are invited to enter your Sacred Space. In that space search the depths of your heart for what you reject the most. Allow your thoughts to wander. Give them permission to go into the dark places within you where you struggle. Do not be afraid of the thoughts. Do not fear the feelings. They are part of you. They make you who you are in the family of God.

Allow the thoughts, the feelings to be themselves. Jesus is with you listening to the thoughts, experiencing the feelings. You find yourself wondering why after so many years these thoughts and feelings still activate anger, frustration and disappointment within. You wonder why after all that has transpired, you still carry each memory with clarity as if it had only occurred yesterday. You shake your head in disbelief. If only you could remember the things you need to remember so clearly...

Jesus calls you to his side. He places his arm around your shoulders. He knows you truly want to be released from all that keeps you from going deeper and experiencing true oneness, total wholeness. Jesus remains present to you. He does not disappear from your midst. He knows you desire to hear his message of love, his promise of union with the Father. He knows you would not meet him in this space if you were not ready. He desires to bless you, to forgive you, to release all that troubles you.

Jesus leads you through the memories of each experience. He anoints each memory with his love. He illuminates your heart with compassion for all involved. He blesses the words that have caused difficulty. He caresses unexpected diagnoses. He applies the balm of forgiveness to the areas that cause you the most turmoil. You feel lighter.

You feel capable of moving through this moment. Divine grace restores your sense of harmony with all of creation.

You thank Jesus for remaining by your side. You thank him for gifting you with the grace of this experience. You offer that same gift of grace for all who struggle. You bless all of creation and give thanks for the gift of Life.

FORGIVENESS

From the heart of Jesus: Matthew 18: 21-35

"...Lord, when my brother wrongs me, how often must I forgive him? Seven times? No, Jesus replied, not seven times; I say, seventy times seven times."

Reflection: At the time of Jesus, the religious Law which governed people's lives offered prescriptions for every aspect of life including forgiveness. Jesus was very familiar with religious Law. He knew following The Law could be a way into holiness for his people, as well as a major obstacle to their growth as people of God. When asked about the act of forgiveness, Jesus elevated the prescription of The Law to the next level by saying forgiveness is limitless. Not only did he talk about forgiveness, but often offered forgiveness as part of his healing process. He offered forgiveness in concrete form, another quality of the One he called Father in order to bring people closer to their True Selves.

Invitation: You are invited to enter your Sacred Space for the purpose of activating Jesus' ability to forgive within your self. The forgiveness that Jesus speaks of is unconditional. It is not predicated upon conditions such as "if you apologize, I'll forgive you...if you admit you were wrong, I'll forgive you...if you make amends and restore peace in the family, I'll forgive you." No, the forgiveness Jesus speaks of is forgiveness for the sake of, for the beauty of restoring harmony, wholeness, a sense of worthiness within the heart of the person who lived and acted in a manner that was less than expected. The forgiveness Jesus speaks of is forgiveness without expectation.

Jesus invites you to receive within your heart and mind his ability to forgive. He gives this gift freely. He gives this gift out of the desire to make you more one with him. He realizes you can not fully identify with him until you are able to experience this level of forgiveness for yourself. Jesus forgave fully because he needed people to forgive him. He needed Mary's forgiveness when he left home to follow his heart in search of the Father. He needed the Baptist's forgiveness when John was murdered over his association with him. He needed the forgiveness of Martha and Mary when he dallied instead of coming immediately to save Lazarus. He needed the forgiveness of Peter, James and John when he led them up the mountain and didn't prepare them for his Transfiguration. Jesus forgave fully because he needed to be forgiven. Jesus forgave fully because he knew he was asking people to align themselves with him when they were not yet ready to understand the mystery he was calling them to. Jesus forgave fully and, at the same time, revealed his need to be forgiven.

In the spirit of Jesus' forgiveness, allow yourself to forgive all. Allow yourself to understand the mystery of all the people who have caused you pain. Forgive yourself for expecting more from them. Forgive your own inability to forgive. Accept Jesus' forgiveness. Offer Jesus' forgiveness as your own. Give thanks and bless this moment.

GROWTH

From the Heart of Jesus: Matthew 5:17-19

"I have come, not to abolish The Law and the prophets, but to fulfill them."

Reflection: Jesus recognized the importance of the past and where that past had led his people. He recognized the validity of the prescription of The Law and the challenges of the prophets who had come before him to affect people's lives. He saw every means of drawing people closer to God as good.

Jesus didn't come to destroy the past. He came to lead people deeper into the heart of God to experience oneness. He came to take people to the next level of humanity where they lived in harmony, not only with their friends, but also with those who waged war against them. He came to those who encountered sickness, limitation, oppression and offered an alternative—the grace of new life, the healing energy of new possibilities. He came to fulfill all the hopes, dreams and desires of God as manifested through His people.

Invitation: You are invited to enter your Sacred Space. In that space Jesus is sitting in the center waiting for you to join him. You sit by his side and wait for him to speak the first word. The silence calms you. The stillness encircles you. You realize there is no need for words at this moment. You feel Jesus' love moving directly into your heart. You acknowledge the connection and rest in that feeling of deep love.

Jesus' love shows you that all things are possible. His love reveals that healing, peace, connection, relationships, abundance, presence are all part of God's design, are all part of the fulfillment of God's deepest desire for oneness with His people. Jesus' love, that moves so freely from his heart, to the space of your heart, reveals the fact that there is no separation, only oneness. You begin to understand. You begin to embrace this mystery.

Jesus asks you to invite others to sit in this same space. He desires that they too share what you and he have shared. You think of many in need. As you recall their names, their situations, they appear and sit with you and Jesus. They too call on others and the room becomes filled. Words are not spoken. Jesus gifts them with love, with healing, with peacefulness, with wonder, with joy. More people arrive and Jesus encourages the group to do for others, as he has done for them. He encourages them in love to live from this state of connection, from a position of oneness, of divine grace and to move from past limitations to the fulfillment of all needs. He invites them to share God's grace and blessings so that all would know the blessings the prophets truly desired for God's people. He invites them to mobilize their compassion and divinely-inspired love and goodness, to bring peace and harmony into all situations. The room resonates with possibilities. This is a new moment for all, a holy moment. Bless this moment and express sincere gratitude for experiencing life as God meant it to be lived, in oneness, in wholeness, in total, perfect union.

ALIGNMENT

From the heart of Jesus: Luke 11: 14-23

"He who is not with me is against me, and he who does not gather with me scatters."

Reflection: Jesus continues with his message of harmony and oneness. He asks people to align themselves with his way of thinking, his way of living so they may experience all he has experienced. He doesn't say the way is easy. After all, his followers were witness to those who rejected his message, his call to enter more deeply into the experience of oneness with God.

Jesus needs the energy of the people. He needs their belief in harmony, in oneness, to touch others. He tells them in no uncertain terms if they aren't with him, they defeat the purpose of his message by splintering the energy, by depleting its power. Jesus encourages all to align their lives with one another in harmony in order to experience oneness, wholeness.

Invitation: You are invited to enter your Sacred Space. In that space you hear the sound of water cascading down the rocks. Your curiosity leads you closer to the water. There you witness the beauty of flowing water, droplets coming together forming a stream. You realize the harmony present among the droplets. You watch as they move together in a continuous flow. The moment stirs your mind and touches your heart. The constant flow of water softens the rocks; over time it smoothes all their rough edges. The journey of the water over the rocks seems effortless. The water and rocks appear in harmony with one another. You watch the beauty of harmony, and at the same time, feel part of it.

You raise your eyes and suddenly see Jesus. He too is one with the water and the rocks. He too is transformed by their beautiful exchange of motion. You stand next to him and understand how everything must work together for overall harmony and balance. You see how every aspect of life is connected. You understand that people need to work together for the benefit of all. You understand that Jesus came to bring this message and now he imparts that same message to you in a deeper way.

Jesus invites you to embrace the message of aligning your energy, your interests, your desires, with God's desires for total union with all people for the benefit of all. You find your heart responding to this invitation. You want to be part of this movement toward wholeness. You want to be a bearer of peace, of harmony, of connection.

You allow Jesus to explain how he needs you to touch others. You listen and realize that your whole life has prepared you for this moment. You will no longer allow conflict to distract you. You will focus your attention on caring for all who surround you— the sick, the poor, the lonely, the broken hearted, those most in need of your understanding. Feel Jesus touch your heart and gift you with the grace of compassion for others. Confirm your desire to work with Jesus for the benefit of others and give thanks for this experience.

EXCITEMENT

From the heart of Jesus: Mark 12: 28-34

"You are not far from the reign of God."

Reflection: Some people heard the message of Jesus and immediately understood. They were ready for his message. They were open. They were looking for a new way of living, a new way of being.

Jesus' message resonated within their hearts because the message was already there. Jesus was able to help them identify the thoughts of harmony, wholeness, union with the Father, and integrate them with the aspects of daily life.

Jesus found comfort in those who understood his message. He realized the time of God had arrived not only in himself, but in those who embraced his words. He grew excited about the possibilities for others. No longer would they live as a people oppressed; before them stood opportunities for abundant life.

Invitation: You are invited to enter your Sacred Space and watch as Jesus speaks to a group of people about the desires of God for His people. There is a sparkle in Jesus' eyes as he speaks about the Father. He wants everyone in the room to know the Father's dreams and desires in the same way that he does. He wants them to know that all they have hoped for, prayed for, waited for in the form of a Messiah is already within their reach, their opportunity.

Jesus shares his energy, his love for an alternate way of living. The way of Jesus is a way of seeing all as one. It is a way of seeing all as in connection with the Source. Jesus tells them to be themselves, to act from their True Selves and to expect all the resources, the blessings of the Father to be present to them. Jesus tells them to call on the Father's blessing as they help others. It is difficult for some to understand. They still are mired in illness, in poverty, in oppression. But Jesus' desire to make them whole is stronger than any limitation. They feel Jesus' desire. You feel his desire to make the entire room one with the Father.

You are invited by Jesus to share the blessings you have received with the group. You hesitate at first, but then begin to recount the moments of connection with the Father via prayer, people, nature, experiences, etc. In that moment, you see how simple it is to be one, how effortless, how natural. Jesus encourages others to do the same. The room is filled with stories of love, of mercy, of kindness, of healing.

Jesus invites all to open the Sacred Space for those in need of wholeness, in need of healing. Love, mercy, kindness and healing fill the space. Those in need realize that there really is no need, no lack, no want. Blessings of mercy are always available to them and for others. Need does not exist. Unconditional blessing, health, and mercy is reality. The room takes on a different feeling. Everyone begins to see what living in God is like. All rest in the ease of oneness, the acceptance of all as it is. You realize that this is life within the heart of God. This is what Jesus has tried to share all along. You reflect and give thanks that you have been given this gift to share with others.

SELF PERCEPTION

From the heart of Jesus: Luke 18: 9-14

"O God, be merciful to me."

Reflection: Jesus offered a parable to reinforce a message. He tells a story of a Pharisee and Tax Collector. The Pharisees imposed their positions of importance upon the people. The Tax Collectors normally kept a portion of the tax they collected for personal benefit and were not respected by the people.

Jesus not only shared their way of praying, but also offered a glimpse of their self-perception and how they had hoped to be seen by God. The Tax Collector asks for mercy. He knows his limitations. He hopes to find forgiveness in the face of God. He offers his heart in a position of receptivity believing that God would see him for what he could be, rather than what he was because of his position. Jesus offers a lesson in humility, a true posture of prayer. Jesus offers a lesson in healing—all healing begins in the heart.

Invitation: You are invited to enter the Sacred Space. In that space you immediately feel the presence of Jesus. You are touched by the thought that healing begins in the heart. You reach out to Jesus and take his hand. You place his hand over your heart.

You cover his hand with your hand. You allow yourself to feel grace flowing into all the areas of your being. You sense a feeling of connection, an overwhelming feeling of mercy. Mercy flows within you. Compassion wells from the depths of your being.

You look into the eyes of Jesus and wonder how this moment of healing could be so vivid. You wonder how you can truly feel all that you are feeling. Jesus smiles as he looks at you. You begin to laugh. You already know that this moment is meant to be shared. You already know that this moment is not meant just for your benefit.

Jesus begins to walk with you toward a small hill. You know deep within there will be people on the other side of the hill waiting for Jesus. You now know that Jesus will expect you to gift others with the grace you have received. Part of you desires to hold on to the grace-filled moment. The other part of you realizes it must be shared.

Parents approach with their children. They appear so sick, so close to death. You reach out immediately and surround each child with the grace of mercy, the grace of fullness of life. You speak words of encouragement to the parents. You hold their hearts in your hand. They come in total humility desiring only wholeness for their children. You tell them there is grace enough for this moment.

You see Jesus from the corner of your eye blessing, healing, touching another group. They too desire only life, only another chance for their child. Jesus looks into their eyes and encourages them. He tells them the Father also wants only what is best for all His children. Jesus tells them that the Father is merciful, the Father is kind. The Father gifts each parent with life for their children. He asks them to trust the mercy of the Father and live within that mercy. He asks them to offer mercy to whatever causes their child distress. Acknowledge that mercy flows from all and give thanks for life.

TRANSFORMATION

From the heart of Jesus: John 9: 1-41

"As he walked along, he saw a man who had been blind from birth. His disciples asked him, Rabbi, was it his sin or that of his parents that caused him to be born blind? Neither, answered Jesus: It was no sin, either of this man or his parents. Rather it was to let God's works show forth in him."

Reflection: Jesus came to dispel the concept that illness and infirmity were a punishment from God. He told his disciples that any unpleasant circumstance, any challenge can be transformed by the love of God in order to manifest the true nature of God. The transition to Jesus' way of thinking on the part of the disciples would require much effort. They would need to adopt Jesus' mindset, rather than the belief system of their ancestors.

Jesus brought the concept of God's ability to work among God's people to a new level. He presented God as Restorer.

Invitation: You are invited to enter the Sacred Space to experience God as the Restorer. Jesus knows that you are open now to any experience he has invited you to share. He knows you have trusted him every step of this journey. Jesus invites you to release any and all belief systems that offer cause and effect scenarios. You realize the request is difficult, especially because you know of a child who is not responding to antibiotics and is within hours of death. Jesus feels your concern for this child and all children who are dying around the globe.

Jesus invites you to welcome the child into the Sacred Space. You carry the child in your heart. Jesus welcomes her presence. He looks deeply into her being. He calls her by name. He realizes her weakness, but does not let it deter him. He touches her heart.

She begins to stir. He fills her with grace, with strength, with life. He searches for her family. Her mother moves toward his side.

Jesus feels the mother's fatigue and hopelessness. He speaks to her of God as Restorer. The mother wants to believe so much in a God who will restore her child to fullness, to vitality after watching her child suffer so much. The mother begs Jesus to breathe life, to speak life into her child. Jesus encourages the mother to do the same. They speak words of restoration, words of hope and words of a future filled with good experiences. The child responds. The child understands the God of Restoration. The child feels God-ness, goodness moving through her being. The child feels a life-force moving through her.

The child encourages other children to seek God the Restorer. They come in the arms of their parents, carried by those who love them. Their hearts become one heart and they feel the connection to Jesus who desires to share life with them. Jesus desires to gift them with God's blessing of health, of life, of peace, of joy. Jesus encourages all to do the same. All touch those in need. All proclaim words of life. All resound with feelings of God blessing everyone in the moment. Cherish the moment. Express gratitude to God for the ability to share this moment with all children in need.

HEART SENSE

From the heart of Jesus: John 4:43-54

"Jesus told him, 'Return home. Your son will live.' "

Reflection: Throughout the miracle stories in scripture, people came to Jesus with requests for themselves and for others. In this case, a father approached Jesus on behalf of his son. The father knew that Jesus was able to assist his son; otherwise he would not have journeyed to Jesus with his request. Jesus knew the hearts of all who approached him. His heart entered their hearts. He knew the depth of this father's love for his son. So Jesus sent him home with the assurance his son would live. The father did not question. He knew beyond fact, beyond faith that the words of Jesus were enough to energize his son. Intuitively, the father knew Jesus' grace and energy could transcend distance and renew life in his son. So he went home and expected his son to greet him upon his arrival.

Invitation: You are invited to enter your Sacred Space. In that space, remember all the times you had prayed for your own child or had been asked to pray for someone else's child. Give thanks for the many opportunities you had been given to enter deeper within yourself and unite yourself in love with all those who offer prayers for children. Remember how grateful you were when the child you were praying for recovered and was able to make noise or run around the house. Allow the memories to bring a smile to your face.

Jesus sees you smiling. He too knows what it feels like to see the relief of parents upon their child's recovery. He knows what it feels like to see a child healthy and playing with friends. Jesus walks toward you. He knows you know that the heart sees everything as it truly is. He knows you know healing is seeing all children as they truly are—vibrant loving expressions of divine life.

In the Sacred Space Jesus reaches out to welcome all children in need of healing.

You are invited to welcome the children with Jesus. You look into their eyes and sense all they want is to be free from hunger, illness, war.

You feel the cries of their hearts—all they desire is to be free from loneliness, ridicule, torment.

Their parents accompany them. Jesus touches their hearts and minds. He gives them grace to walk with their children into the future. He offers hope in the midst of difficult situations. They trust Jesus. They know he sees something they can't yet see. They know he lives believing in harmony, oneness and connection with the Father.

They hold onto Jesus' belief for them and their children. They embrace the future.

You touch the shoulder of each parent and child offering reassurance. In your heart you give thanks that each encounter can bring hope and freedom. You feel Jesus' heart with your own heart and give thanks.

DESIRE

From the heart of Jesus: John 5:1-16

"Do you want to be healed?"

Reflection: A man with a chronic illness sat at the poolside in Bethseda known for its miraculous properties. Jesus approached him while he was waiting with the group to be placed in the healing waters. Jesus asked the man if he wanted to be healed. The man must have thought what a ridiculous question. Would he be here waiting for assistance into the pool if he didn't want to be healed? But Jesus wanted the man to articulate his need. Jesus needed the man to identify and to proclaim what he needed most.

Instead of helping the man into the pool, Jesus told him to stand up, pick up the mat he was resting on, and walk! Jesus stirred the pool of grace present within the man to activate the energy necessary for healing. Jesus showed the man that what he most desired was already inside him.

Invitation: You are invited to enter your Sacred Space and think about the areas of your life in need of healing. You are invited to ask yourself if you really want to feel whole, if you really want to lead a life filled with joy, excitement and the promise of a vibrant future. If you do desire to feel fully alive, proclaim that desire in the Sacred Space. If you really want to be healed, say so. Speak the words out loud numerous times so that they resonate within your being and feel natural. Fill the Sacred Space with your desire to be one with Jesus, one with those who love you, one with all of creation. Reach deep within your being until all you know is wholeness, oneness, healing.

You are invited to open your eyes and see Jesus. He is standing near you at this moment in your Sacred Space. He understands what it took for you to delve within your heart and mind and proclaim wholeness. He knows what it took for you to put aside your fears, to abandon your pain and proclaim your True Self, your real identity—a person, one with him and all of creation, who chooses to be alive.

Jesus walks toward you and asks what you desire most at this moment.

You wonder if you should really bare your heart and tell him. You feel a little awkward, but begin to speak. Jesus senses your hesitancy and takes your hands into his. A sense of calm fills your being. You begin to feel as if Jesus is already responding to your needs. You feel his power, his love, his kindness moving through your being. You begin to feel peaceful within. You begin to see yourself with new eyes.

You think of all the people close to you and the needs they also have. You share those needs with Jesus and he asks you to see them through new eyes. You see them healed. You see them in fruitful relationships. You see them at peace, filled with a sense of calm within. You see them moving through life with the freedom and joy of their youth. They look happy. Their eyes are radiant. You hold their hearts in your heart and give thanks for the ability to see them as they truly are. Continue to give thanks.

TRUTH

From the heart of Jesus: John 5: 17-30

"My Father is at work until now, and I am at work as well."

Reflection: Those in power were beginning to grow more upset with Jesus' words and actions. Jesus had an answer for them that further raised their level of anger. Jesus put himself on the same level as the Father. He performed miracles on the Sabbath, even though work was not permitted on the Sabbath. He informed the group that the Father was constantly at work offering grace, abundance and healing. Jesus assured them that he too would minister to the people whenever they were in need. The powerful could not understand. They knew only The Law. The Law was their path into abundance, blessing, and acceptance. The Law would take preference over the people.

Jesus challenged their thought processes and belief systems. Despite their inability to understand what he was all about, Jesus continued to work, to manifest the qualities of God that restored life. Despite their inability to accept his message, Jesus continued to speak from his heart and expose them to the grace of the Father.

Invitation: You are invited to join Jesus in your Sacred Space. The crowds are already gathered there. You are the last to arrive. The crowds are pressing in on Jesus. They need him to meet their needs. He desires to do so. He desires that you too reach within the goodness of your self and respond with hope, with compassion, with divine grace.

The people move toward you for a touch, a word, a gesture, a response to their needs. You feel comfortable providing for them. You know that this is a treasured moment. You realize that Jesus is asking you to share in the work that he came to accomplish. You feel capable listening as people unburden themselves. You distribute clothes from your own supply to those without. You prepare and serve food for the hungry.

You speak with the lonely. You comfort those who have lost a loved one.

Jesus looks at you and realizes that you have identified with him and with the Father. Jesus realizes you now know the truth. You no longer see needs as overwhelming. You simply gather the available resources to meet the needs of others. You are confident that you will be able to be present, to be a sign of God's love and unconditional caring for his people. You encourage others to do the same. You call their hearts to respond in the same manner that Jesus' heart called your heart. People in need present an opportunity to identify with God's abundant love. Their needs become the catalyst for the manifestation of divine caring.

More people desire to share divine love and caring with others. They too heal, listen, clothe, feed, nurture, console and bring hope to the crowds. Jesus realizes that his message is being embraced and embodied by this crowd of people hungry for divine intervention, divine interaction. Jesus realizes that all begin to grasp the truth. This is a holy moment of reconciliation, a moment of truth. Give thanks for the moment.

ON BEHALF OF

From the heart of Jesus: John 5: 31-47

"I have come in my Father's name, yet you do not accept me."

Reflection: In the time of Jesus, whenever a son introduced himself, he did not do so using his own name, but the name of his father. The people were expected to extend the same welcome to the son as they would the father.

Jesus applied this same principle to his heavenly Father, indicating that he was coming on behalf of, or in the name of his heavenly Father. This concept was too much for the people in authority. To them, Jesus was a man like each of them. To them he could not claim any special connection to the Father.

Jesus agreed. He was the same as they were. Therefore they too could introduce themselves as children of the Father and expect to be welcomed in the same way the Father would be welcomed. They could expect to receive and impart all the blessings of the Father.

Invitation: You are invited to enter your Sacred Space. In that space recall the many opportunities you've had in your life to welcome others or to be welcomed by them.

Remember also the numerous times you've had to extend greetings on behalf of a family member or friend who could not be present during a special event, but had asked you to let the others know that they were being thought of. Recall how seriously you relayed their message, how deeply you desired to make their intentions felt. Allow those memories to occupy a space in your heart and be a gentle reminder of what it is like to present yourself on behalf of someone else.

Jesus enters the Sacred Space and watches you cradle the memories within your being. He moves closer to you and asks you share the time you were most moved when you bestowed greetings on behalf of someone else. You share the moment. Jesus realizes you know now how he felt each and every time he spoke, touched, healed on behalf of the Father. Jesus invites you to enter his level of intimacy with the Father. In that space he asks you to greet every person, every situation as if you are the messenger, the outward sign of the Father. He asks you to think as the Father would think, to feel as the Father would feel, to respond as the Father would respond to people's needs. You think from your heart. You respond from a sense of freedom. Your whole being sees only possibilities, only the limitless nature of potentiality.

You find yourself desiring to be the manifestation of all that the Father is and could be for people if only they could see the Father through the eyes of Jesus and now through your eyes as well: the Father—Creator, Coordinator, Collaborator with and for the good of all. You find yourself transported beyond the Sacred Space to all the areas of the world where people are in need. You see yourself with Jesus in hospitals and hospices. You hear yourself with Jesus offering peaceful solutions to numerous conflict-ridden areas. You feel yourself with Jesus offering mercy to people who can not even forgive themselves. You bless, you console, you feed, you touch all in need in the name of the Father. You give thanks for this life-changing experience.

PRESENCE

From the heart of Jesus: John 7: 1-2, 10, 25-30

"I know him because it's from him I come: He sent me."

Reflection: Jesus knew his heavenly Father. He knew he flowed from the same energy, creativity, essence and consciousness that was the Father. Jesus knew the heavenly Father sent him on behalf of Himself. Jesus knew the heavenly Father needed to make Himself more present to people in order for people to tap into that same consciousness of the Father to experience oneness.

The sense of knowing he was sent by the heavenly Father empowered Jesus. He desired to empower others with the message that all he was, they too could be. He wanted them to feel the presence of the heavenly Father within them. He knew they could if they just would be attentive. He wanted them to feel the Father waiting to be invited into the situations that caused them the most concern.

Invitation: You are invited to enter your Sacred Space. In that space recall a time when you felt the presence of someone who loved you. Try to remember as much about the person's love for you. Try to remember what the person said, what the person did to make you feel that you were totally loved by him or her. Hold the memories deep within your being. Recall how you felt totally alive, totally one with life because of the person's love for you. Remember how you thought all was possible because of the person's love for you and belief in you. Allow those memories to empower you. Allow those memories to stir new life within you.

Jesus invites you, empowered by the memories of deep love, to join him near the fire.

You walk toward the flames and the memories of abiding, loving presence burn deeper within you. You feel renewed and refreshed. Jesus realizes you are ready to experience the presence of the Father in a more profound manner now. You've been prepared by memories of love to experience the Father and the Father's love.

Jesus knew love was the way the Father reached out to all. Jesus knew love was the way to the Father.

The flames call you closer. You feel a presence. It is familiar. You feel at home, at peace in this gentle knowing. The presence is old, yet in some way, new. The presence is so much like Jesus that you wonder if it truly is Jesus. It can't be though because you see Jesus with your eyes. He stands before you. The presence draws you to Himself. He wraps His arms around you. He cradles your head in the palm of His hand as you rest your head on His shoulder. You know beyond doubt that the presence is the Father. You know within your heart, within your soul, with all your being that the Father has gifted you with this intimate knowledge of Himself. You know and you want to share this knowledge with others as Jesus desired to share it with you. You call people to approach the fire. They do so without fear. They've watched the Father embrace you and desire that same embrace. You accompany them to the Father with Jesus. You pour out your love for their concerns and cares. You bless them and give thanks that you have been allowed to lead them to the Father.

THIRST

From the heart of Jesus: John 7: 40-53

"...No man ever spoke like that before."

Reflection: Now even the temple guards realized Jesus was not like any one else they had ever heard. They were jeered and taunted by the chief priests and Pharisees for taking an interest in him, for paying attention to his words.

But Jesus' message was seeping into the hearts of those most ready to receive it. The energy behind Jesus' words gravitated to people filled with a similar energy. They were able to relate to thirsting for something more. They desired the oneness Jesus spoke of. They were open because The Law did not bind them. They saw Jesus as capable of taking them places The Law had not taken them. They saw Jesus as the culmination of all they aspired to, rather than a force of destruction, or an agent of separation. Jesus' words were new to them and caused their hearts to stir with his message.

Invitation: You are invited to enter your Sacred Space. In that space you see Jesus seated along the banks of a flowing stream. You see people gathering around to listen to Jesus' message. You can feel their thirst. You sense their hunger. They desire to receive all that Jesus has to give.

You find yourself slowly walking toward the crowd. As you approach the stream you are caught up by the way the water flows so freely over the rocks. It appears as if the water is providing nourishment to each rock and the bottom of the stream. You allow your mind to wander. There is so much thirsting within you, within your family, within your network of friends. There are so many needs just waiting to be quenched by the Living Waters that flow from the heart, mind and spirit of Jesus.

You make your way toward Jesus and wonder if you have ever heard him speak so powerfully. You are caught up in his excitement. You are caught up in his connection to the Father. You've felt that same excitement before. You've experienced connection with the Father before—all because of the time you've spent with Jesus.

You carry the "thirsts" of everyone you know in your heart. You carry their sickness, their pain, their broken relationships, their longing for something more. You desire that their "thirsts" are quenched by the Ever-Living, Ever-Loving Father. The Father senses your desire to see them as they truly are, to see them whole. You carry your own "thirst", your own longing for something more. You realize that "thirsts" and "longings" are opportunities to move beyond the present situation. You are grateful for being entrusted with these keys to unlock your heart and to unblock your mind. You are thankful for all the streams of your life and the lives of others. You realize that the "thirsts" that lead to Jesus and the Father begin with Jesus and the Father. You realize the "thirsts" are just another way to bring you back to your True Self.

Bless all the "thirsts". Bless all the situations that call for a Divine Response and give thanks.

CONSCIOUSNESS

From the heart of Jesus: John 11: 1-45

"This sickness is not to end in death; rather it is for God's glory."

Reflection: When Jesus received word from Martha and Mary that Lazarus was sick, he assured his followers that the sickness would not end in death, but be used to reveal God's glory. Jesus would show them that the glory of God would be manifested in the compassion extended to Lazarus, as well as Martha and Mary. The glory of God would not be so much the raising of Lazarus from the dead, but the coming together of all who loved Lazarus and his family so that no one would feel alone or betrayed. Jesus was already preparing his friends and followers for the compassion needed in the coming days—the support they would need to be for one another when Jesus would be taken from them by death. To raise Lazarus took little effort on the part of Jesus. To raise people's consciousness to stand together in the midst of fear, in the midst of despair would be a true sign of God's glory.

Invitation: You are invited to move into your Sacred Space and make your way toward the place within you that feels most in need of life. You reflect upon what has caused this intense lack of vitality. You refrain from judging the words, the actions, the inaction that has brought you to this moment. You simply trust that the experience was necessary for you to rise to a new level of understanding. You are invited to allow yourself to feel compassion for the part of you that has died.

Jesus calls your name and you look into his eyes. You feel more alive. Jesus called your name as you were offering compassion to yourself. You wonder if he knew you were about to cry. Your mind wanders. Is this is how Lazarus felt deep inside the tomb? You wonder if Lazarus' spirit was waiting for Jesus to call his name. You wonder if Lazarus was waiting for any one to call his name. You are caught up in the wonder of the moment. You are caught up in the connection between yourself and Lazarus. You wonder if Lazarus' story is the story of all people who need someone to call their name, to call them into new life.

Jesus knows you have broken through the barrier of self and moved into the realm of consciousness where you feel connected not only with Lazarus, but with all people in need. He knows you now know how important it is to call people out of their tombs and into new life, new opportunities, into hope for this moment, tomorrow and beyond.

Jesus invites you to call the names of people most in need. He invites you to offer compassion, empathy and gentleness. He invites you to stand by them in their fear and longing. He invites you to help them rise from the depths of their despair. He invites you to help them see that they are not alone. Each time someone rises, the glory of God fills the room. Each time someone transcends his/her limitations, God's glory is magnified. Feel glory fill the room. Feel glory fill their lives. Bless this moment of realization. Give thanks for this moment of connection to the Divine.

FAITHFULNESS

From the heart of Jesus: John 8: 1-11

"Woman, where did they all disappear to?"

Reflection: The scribes and Pharisees brought Jesus a woman caught in adultery. They did so to trap him, hoping he would provide an answer contrary to The Law. Jesus turned the tables on the group and encouraged those who had never sinned to throw the first stone. One by one, they disappeared.

Jesus felt the heart of humiliation in the woman before him. He identified with her in her moment of embarrassment, her time of pain. Jesus didn't chastise. He did not condemn. He encouraged her to be faithful to her true identity—one with God. By his love, he drew her to see herself from a position of love. By his love, he invited her to see herself through the eyes of the heavenly Father—in total freedom, peace, and harmony.

Invitation: You are invited to enter your Sacred Space. Jesus is waiting there for you. You sense his presence yet do not see him. As you move toward the center of the room your eyes meet the eyes of Jesus. His heart is sad. His eyes are filled with tears. You wonder what has caused his pain. You reach out to him and he appreciates your gesture of concern. You look over his shoulder and see what causes him so much pain. There are so many people waiting for Jesus. They have been embarrassed by others. Their hearts have been ripped apart by the judgment of others. They are in need of validation. They are in need of love. Jesus identifies with their needs. You realize their pain is his pain. You realize his pain is your pain at this moment.

Jesus takes a deep breath and encourages you to do the same. You sense he is about to approach the people. He gestures for them to follow him toward the hills. They do so moving as one body. Walking up the hill Jesus stops to caress the fragile branches of a small tree. He encourages you to do the same. The people imitate the gesture. At the top of the hill Jesus sits down. He begins to speak about knowing who you really are. He shares that all are like branches of the small, fragile tree. All need a gentle touch, encouragement to grow, water, sun and fertile soil to be who they need to be.

All need freedom to be able to breathe, to realize who they truly are.

Jesus invites the people to breathe the air of freedom. He invites them to move beyond the words, the limitations, the taunts of others. He asks them to live fully in this new moment. They look at him with eyes wide open. They want all that he speaks of. They want to feel alive, to feel loved, to be valued. They desire to share those same sentiments with others. Encouraged by Jesus, they speak to one another. They proclaim all that is good within.

The people are reminded to be faithful to their True Selves. Jesus encourages them to draw that self out of others who suffer from judgment and humiliation. You acknowledge the beauty of the moment and give thanks.

ONENESS

From the heart of Jesus: John 8: 21-30

"The one who sent me is with me. He has not deserted me."

Reflection: Jesus is challenged once again by those who do not believe in him. First he tells them that the world they belong to can not hold him. That world is not big enough. His spirit needs the open space of the celestial realm to soar. But they do not understand because they live bound by fear and limited perspectives.

Jesus further tells them that the one who sent him, the heavenly Father, is always with him, is as much a part of him as his very self. Jesus reiterates that the same heavenly Father has not abandoned him, even though so many are not receptive to the message he brings. Jesus reinforces the fact that the Father and he are one. Jesus reveals that same oneness to all who will open the eyes of their hearts to see.

Invitation: You are invited to enter your Sacred Space. Soft lights glow in the space and gentle instrumental music plays in the background. You are drawn to the music. The tender notes open your heart. Jesus walks toward you and gently touches your heart. He desires to share all that is in his heart with your heart.

You sit next to Jesus and he encourages you to see the presence of the Father in all circumstances. He invites you to let your spirit soar and connect with the Father.

You allow the music to open your heart, your mind and your spirit. You feel connected to everything and everyone. You feel a connection to the Father. You wonder if this is what Jesus feels, what he means when he speaks about being always in tune, always one with the Father.

You allow the music to penetrate your being creating connection upon connection. You see circumstances, situations, people pass before you. You invite them to allow the music to connect them to the heart of the Father. You realize that this sense of connection must be shared. It can not be contained or hidden just for your benefit. You understand in that moment why Jesus needed to share his experience with others. You understand in a new way why connection with the Father was so central to the message of Jesus. The Father was the spark which ignited the fire within the being of Jesus. The Father's goodness, grace, energy propelled Jesus into action, would not allow Jesus to remain still or quiet even in the face of resistance. The Father's message was Jesus' message. The Father's message is now your message.

You are encouraged to embody the message for yourself and your own situations. You are empowered to share the message of constant companionship with others.

People are drawn into the Sacred Space by the music. They come to hear that they are not alone. They come to hear that the Father is present within their needs. They come to find companionship, healing, inner peace and resolution of their concerns. They are ready to be freed from the limitations that have constrained them and desire to move into the realm of possibility. This is their moment of realization. It is your moment of watching oneness in action. Embrace the moment and give thanks.

FREEDOM

From the heart of Jesus: John 8: 31-42

"...if the Son frees you, you will really be free."

Reflection: Jesus challenged the people's belief system once again. They claimed to be the free children of Abraham, yet still did not identify with the message Jesus tried to share with them.

Jesus tried to break through their barriers, their misconceptions of The Law and show them what true freedom was—identification with the Father. They were not ready. They believed themselves to be the children of Abraham and could not transcend that relationship. They could not imagine that there was One greater than Abraham who could be present among them, who would care for their needs, who would offer a message of wholeness that would take them further than The Law. Jesus was the Father's presence among them, the Father's representative. Jesus offered words. He acted on their behalf. He tried to show them what their lives could be like if only they would open themselves to other options. He gifted them with grace, all with the hope that they would know freedom by identification with the Father and find true liberation.

Invitation: You are invited to enter your Sacred Space. In that space, you are invited to remember a time when you felt totally free, totally unencumbered by thoughts, feelings, or circumstances. Allow yourself to re-live that time. Remember how the present and the future appeared so open, so abundant, with so much promise. Remember the dreams and desires you had to contribute to the good of humanity, to touch lives, to offer love and caring. Remain in that space, for in that space, you remember what freedom truly felt like.

Jesus joins you in your Sacred Space. He recognizes the smile on your face as you remember another time, another place when the present and future were filled with joy, excitement and freedom. He remembers your sense of feeling totally alive and desires that you experience those same feelings now and also as you walk with him into the future. He infuses your heart and mind with clarity. He helps you to see the present for what it truly is—an opportunity for wholeness, healing, oneness. He helps you to see that as He is the messenger of the Father for all people, so too are you the messenger of the Father for yourself, your situation and the situations of those you touch by your words and actions. Jesus shows you freedom in this moment—freedom for the present time and freedom for the future.

The door to the Sacred Space opens and a group of people wait outside the door. They stream in slowly looking for Jesus. Jesus welcomes them. They feel at peace. Jesus already knows their needs. Jesus reaches out and assures them that this is a new moment, a moment for hope, a moment for joy, a moment to believe that they are free from all that limits them. He asks you to help encourage the people. You join him. You share a word, a touch, a dream that speaks of hope and freedom. You bless this moment and give thanks for feeling the freedom that comes from this experience.

WISDOM

From the heart of Jesus: John 8: 51-59

"But I know him."

Reflection: Jesus confounded the people with his sense of intimacy with the Father. They could relate to Abraham, but could not associate, nor identify themselves with the heavenly Father that Jesus spoke of. That concept was beyond their imagination.

Jesus truly confused them. He was one of them, yet identified so closely with the heavenly Father and boldly proclaimed his knowledge of that same Father.

The message he came to bring was: the Father and I are one. There is no separation. What the heavenly Father does, so do I do, so too you can do. The Father desires oneness, connection. The heavenly Father cannot imagine separation. The heavenly Father invites all to experience oneness, to live in oneness with him in order to experience limitlessness.

Invitation: You are invited to enter your Sacred Space and walk toward the center of that space. There you will find Jesus waiting for you. He stands near a fountain of flowing water. He cups the water with his hands and begins to drink. He encourages you to do the same. You place your hands under the fountain and enjoy the cool sensation of the water. Your hands linger under the water, feeling refreshed and renewed. You marvel at the experience. You wonder what you will feel like once you actually drink from this fountain.

Jesus encourages you to drink. You cup your hands and bring the water toward your face. You drink and feel grateful for this gift. Jesus speaks to you of the Father. He compares his identification with the Father to the water from this fountain. He shares that the Father enlivens him and refreshes him. Jesus indicates that as the water becomes part of his life, your life, so too the Father is part of his life and your life. He shares that the Father can not be separated from any of his children or any part of creation. He shares that the

Father knows no limitations, knows only how to give over and over again from the depths of His being. Jesus indicates that he needs you to drink from this fountain of life giving water in order to be filled with the grace of the Heavenly Father. Jesus desires that you share that same grace with others in need.

You wonder if Jesus' message can be this simple. You wonder if Jesus' message of oneness with the Father is this easy to understand. You trust Jesus and drink more water from the fountain. You desire to know oneness with the Father more deeply. You desire to know the Father as Jesus knows the Father. The image of this fountain, the feelings of being refreshed and renewed remain in your mind. You now have a glimpse of what Jesus speaks of—intimacy, connection, the desire to share oneness with all—because of the oneness the Father has shared with you. This is a holy moment. There is no separation. You hold this moment in your heart and mind. You share the experience with others whenever they need a sense of connection, a sense of oneness. You bless and give thanks for this moment.

EMPOWERMENT

From the heart of Jesus: John 10: 31-42

"...Scripture can not lose its force."

Reflection: With each declaration of who Jesus truly was, those in power grew more concerned. The balance of power was being upset. They were ready to put him to death in order to silence his claims.

Jesus challenged them further. He wanted to know why they were so ready to stone him. He reiterated an important point for his day, as well as future days—scripture cannot lose its energy, cannot lose the power, the intimacy behind it. The multitude of stories, of legends contain life, grace for those who read it time after time. Jesus attempted to impart another message. Go to the scriptures to see, to feel, to embrace the energy of the One known as God. Allow the scriptures to energize and grace all elements of your being.

Invitation: You are invited to enter your Sacred Space and open your heart to the many Scripture readings that have touched you throughout your life. Allow the words and images to flow through your mind. The readings have taken root within your heart and now arise within your memory to be your companion in this space. Hear the words. Feel the emotions. Identify with the characters in each sacred reading. Allow the spirit of the readings to nourish any area within you that is in need. Present your fears, your pain and your wounds. They will be healed by grace found in each sacred reading. Present your dreams, your hopes, your desires for self and others. They will be empowered by abundant love found in each sacred reading. The readings are timeless. The divine grace they impart is limitless. Do not be afraid to share any aspect of your life. The sacred readings wait for you. The sacred readings wait for this moment to minister to you. Go to the Scriptures. Open a page.

Jesus is present in the Sacred Space. He encourages you to allow the readings to empower you. He shares that he himself sought solace and received comfort from the Psalms and the books of the Prophets. He shares that he too felt empowered by the words, by the chanting in the Temple. He shares that he too began to understand his role, his relationship to his people by delving deeper into the Scriptures and allowing them to fill him with grace.

Jesus encourages you to remember any reading that touched your heart. He encourages you to embrace the spirit that flows from the reading. He encourages you to feel one with him, one with the Father, one with all of creation. He sheds light on your mind in order that you may understand the message. He stirs your heart in order that you may embark on a new journey nourished by the holy words. He moves your spirit in order that you feel truly one with the Father and partake in the experience of total abundance, total outpouring of self for the sake of others. This is a sacred moment. You realize that what is being offered to you is pure grace, pure gift—the blessing of ages past, present and to come. You open yourself to receive this gift and give thanks.

NEW APPROACH

From the heart of Jesus: John 11: 45-56

"What are we to do, with this man performing all sorts of signs? If we let him go on like this, the whole world will believe in him."

Reflection: The chief priests and Pharisees called a meeting to discuss why they were letting Jesus get away with all the miraculous signs he performed for the people. They knew if Jesus continued to affect people's lives in this way, he would gain in popularity and they would lose their stronghold over the people.

Their fear was real. The people were not ignorant. As much as they respected The Law and the prescriptions of The Law, Jesus was touching their hearts and minds in a new way. Jesus was offering a way of living that dealt more with identification with a Heavenly Being, rather than fear of that Being. Jesus' message resonated within their hearts. His message found a home within their beings.

Invitation: You are invited to enter your Sacred Space with a sense of expectancy. You are invited to enter the space knowing that you too will receive a miracle from your encounter with Jesus. You enter the space and immediately your heart is filled with love. You are overwhelmed at first, but begin to grow accustomed to being filled with pure love. Jesus' love is there for you. It is the same love that Jesus received from the Father and is happy to share. It is love without expectation. It is love without conditions. It is love from Love.

Jesus moves toward you and begins to speak. He tells you that every situation needs to be filled with love from Love that you just experienced. He tells you that love from Love can restore life, balance, wholeness, goodness to any and all situations. He tells you that this is the approach you need to take with any challenge that comes your way—it is a new approach for you, an approach that leads to miracles—fill each challenge, each situation that causes pain with love from Love. Share the love that you received with others. Encourage them to do the same.

Jesus invites you to sit silently and allow love from Love to fill your being. He invites you to allow love to walk through your memories and replace the anger with love.

He invites you to allow love to heal your body and restore wholeness. He invites you to allow love to heal any aspect of life that cries out for healing. He invites you to allow love to empower all the relationships that bring joy in your life. He invites you to allow love to energize your home, your place of work and anywhere you travel.

Jesus invites you to let people and situations appear before you. You share love from Love with them. People come with broken hearts, cancer diagnoses, lost jobs, foreclosed homes, suicidal children—you find yourself offering an outstretched hand and a word of love. You speak of love from Love. You see their situations bathed in love from Love. You identify with the Father, as Jesus identified with the Father. You realize miracles happen from this heavenly space of love from Love. You feel your heart expand as you offer love from Love. You give thanks for this experience.

SACRED SPACE

From the heart of Jesus: Mark 14: 1-15

"She has done what she could."

Reflection: Jesus ministered to the people of his time. The same people also cared for Jesus' needs. A woman came to anoint Jesus with perfume. She poured it over his head. Those around who did not understand the mutual need to minister as well as be ministered to, commented that this act was a waste of perfume, a waste of money.

Jesus interrupts their comments. He supports the woman's action because she had the courage to live fully from her heart. She knew people would view her action negatively. She didn't let their thoughts or words stop her. She knew she would be the talk of upcoming conversations, but still she did what she had to do. Jesus knew the sacred space she operated from. It was the home of compassion, the place where he also found the courage and strength to act. He reinforced the fact that all actions flow from that same sacred space.

Invitation: You are invited to enter your Sacred Space and watch the woman anoint Jesus' head with perfumed oils. You already know the purpose of the anointing from the Gospel, yet watch in gentle wonder. You see her break open the jar and empty its contents. You smell the perfume as it permeates the room. You hear the comments, sense the negativity and watch the love that streams from the eyes of Jesus. This is a holy moment and you realize this in the deepest part of your being.

You realize the woman knew she would be ridiculed for her actions and chose to love regardless of what others would say. You realize she lived compassion. You realize she was truly empowered by love from Love.

Jesus invites you to break open a jar of perfumed oil that sits next to him. He invites you to pour the oil over him and over the woman. You do so with a heart filled with love. He asks that you give him the jar. He pours oil over your head as well. You feel it touch your scalp and flow into your hair. You feel a connection to Jesus and his sacred moment of anointing in a new way. You feel as if you are being prepared for something more difficult than you have ever experienced. Yet you are confident that Jesus has gifted you with the grace of oil to soften all fear and prepare you for the next moment.

Jesus returns the jar to you. You hold it in your hands as if it contains a secret concerning your future. You stare at the oil and realize it is the oil of compassion, the oil of longing. You desire to share this oil with all in need. You touch people's hearts, minds and spirits with it. You bless their hopes, dreams and desires for the future. You anoint all their broken spaces in need of healing. You caress those who are about to die. You offer oil to the souls of those who have been martyred with certainty that their journey into the heart of God will be one of peace. You comfort those left behind and offer a balm of healing to replace revenge. Jesus speaks words of peace, words of calm and words of restoration. The sacred space becomes a place where everyone lives to minister to others. You bless this moment and give thanks.

RECOGNITION

From the heart of Jesus: John 12: 1-11

"Mary brought a pound of costly perfume made from genuine aromatic nard, with which she anointed Jesus' feet. Then she dried his feet with her hair."

Reflection: John's gospel presents the story of anointing in a slightly different way. However, the message remains—not only do people need to be ministered to, they need to minister, to give of themselves to others. In this case, Mary needed to express her love for Jesus in a tangible way. Often she sat at his feet and listened to his words. She marveled at his raising her brother, Lazarus from the dead. So much emotion, so much gratitude welled up within Mary's heart. Mary needed to let the feelings flow from her and over Jesus so he too could feel that his actions were understood at the deepest level possible within a human context. Mary acted. Jesus understood and allowed himself to be the recipient of her grace.

Invitation: You are invited to enter your Sacred Space and sit in the silence of tremendous love. You close your eyes and allow love to penetrate your whole being. Perfumed oil fills the air. You allow the scent of the oil to lift you beyond the confines of the room. Jesus walks over to you and sits by your side. You feel his love. You feel the depth of his caring. You recognize that the purpose of Jesus' anointing was to enable him to continue to share Love, to continue to Be Love for all people, for all eternity. You recognize that Jesus' anointing was not only for his benefit, but for all people regardless of place and time. You recognize that the oil on his feet would also touch the earth and leave its mark. You realize the oil would sanctify each path taken from that moment on. You acknowledge that the earth is anointed and anoints all who walk in its soil because of its contact with Jesus.

Jesus invites you to walk with him all over the globe. He invites you "to walk the oil of anointing" to areas in need of healing. With

Jesus you walk to villages where children are starving, you walk through makeshift clinics where people are dying from malaria. With Jesus you walk through the fields that long for rain, you walk up mountains that beg for snow. With Jesus you walk beside grieving parents, husbands, wives and children waiting for answers. With Jesus you walk and touch the earth with the "oil of anointing". The oil touches all who touch the earth. The sacred oil prepares them to respond in love to any situation, to every situation.

You recognize that to respond in love to any and all situations requires love from Love. You recognize that this type of love can only come from the Source. Your "walk of anointing" with Jesus confirms that human love is a catalyst of love from Love. Human love can carry Love to places where others may be afraid to go. Jesus shows you that love from Love knows no fear, knows no limitation, knows only a compassionate response. Jesus invites you to share love from Love with everyone who cries for help, with everyone who has any type of need. Jesus invites you to share love from Love for all in pain so that their pain is transformed into Love. You look at each situation with Love, bless it and give thanks.

TRANSCENDING LIMITATIONS

From the heart of Jesus: John 13:21-33, 36-38

"Now is the Son of Man glorified and God is glorified in him."

Reflection: Jesus experienced betrayal by one closest to him. He is saddened by that fact, but also realized that this act will lead him beyond himself. There, Jesus would be asked to live the words he preached. There, he would be asked to surrender into the Divine Mystery. He didn't know if he was capable of that level of surrender.

The gospel states the Son of Man is glorified and God is glorified in him. God is glorified whenever man is true to him or herself. God is glorified whenever people transcend the limitations that prohibit them from the experience of oneness. God is glorified when people reach deep within and connect with the grace of compassion for their needs, as well as the needs of others. God is glorified when people embody compassion.

Invitation: You are invited to enter your Sacred Space. In that space you are invited to recall the many times you have heard the gospel reading that describes Jesus being betrayed by someone close to him. You are invited to enter the heart of Jesus and fully appreciate how this betrayal affected him. In Jesus' heart you begin to understand why Jesus was who he was and how he truly manifested the qualities and responses of the Father.

In the heart of Jesus, you are invited to understand how betrayal is a consequence of fear, a consequence of insecurity. You begin to understand that betrayal really has nothing to do with the person, but more to do with the lack of power the person has over the situation. Judas lacked power over Jesus' actions. Judas could not urge Jesus strongly enough to stand up to those who oppressed their people. Judas could not encourage Jesus to adopt a position of rebellion, rather than a position of availability for all people and their needs.

In the heart of Jesus you begin to understand that forces were at war within the close circle of Jesus' companions—forces of jealousy, forces of alternate ideas for bringing about resolution to the Roman occupation, forces that questioned if they really were following the Messiah or just another man who worked miracles in their midst. Jesus felt their questions, their hesitancy deep within his heart. He carried their burdens in silence. He saw that they were not yet ready to experience the Light. Jesus knew betrayal at its deepest level and let it run its course. In his heart of hearts, Jesus knew he would have enough strength to move beyond betrayal. Jesus knew the acts, the words of betrayal were necessary to take him to the next level.

You identify with Jesus. You remember times you have been betrayed. You remember how the betrayal caused you pain and wounded your spirit. You realize though that the betrayals did not break you. Actually the betrayals freed you to embrace all that came your way. The betrayals liberated you in a manner that helped you to transcend limitations. In the spirit of Jesus, allow yourself to embrace this moment. See yourself walking into the future with Jesus. Bless this moment and give thanks.

UNDERSTANDING

From the heart of Jesus: Matthew 26: 14-25

"The Teacher says: 'My appointed time draws near.'"

Reflection: Jesus knew in his deepest self that every moment of his life, of his ministry, led to this moment. He had to make things right with those closest to him. He had to make certain they really understood why he was here, what he was called to do. He needed them to know his experience of oneness with the Father as their own experience.

He sent the disciples to find a place to share a meal. In taking them to new surroundings, perhaps they would be open in a way that would allow his words to penetrate more deeply? Perhaps they would begin to understand? In taking them out of the familiar, Jesus was offering a glimpse of the depth of love they too would be called to experience. Jesus felt what awaited him. He knew the confusion of the coming hours. Yet Jesus wanted his followers to know he would transcend the experience. He wanted them to embrace the freedom of knowing nothing could stop the love that would be unleashed by his brokenness. He would emerge stronger. His capacity to experience oneness would be enhanced.

Invitation: You are invited to enter your Sacred Space and join Jesus and his apostles in the Upper Room. You already know what awaits the group—the gathering for a meal, the breaking of bread, the questioning, the betrayal, the departure. You know the sequence all too well. You are invited to watch for something you have not yet seen. You are invited to listen for words you have not yet heard.

Jesus joins the group and embraces each one. Jesus embraces you. You realize there is something different about Jesus in this experience of the Sacred Space. He appears sullen. He seems as if he is thinking about the next few hours. He appears consumed by thoughts, by emotions. You sense he is trying to make things "right" in his mind and in his heart. You sense he needs to give of himself

118

totally in this moment so that the apostles will begin to understand what he has spoken about and tried to do in the name of his Father. Your heart feels deeply for Jesus. You want to release the anguish within him. You want to offer him the same compassion that he bestowed on others. Jesus looks your way. He senses you feel his struggle. He knows you know.

Jesus begins to speak to the apostles. His words touch their hearts. He encourages them to remain together, to believe in each other and to care for one another. He encourages them to seek solace in knowing that the Father is as present for them as he is for Jesus. He reminds them that all things are possible when they align themselves with the Father. You realize Jesus holds their hearts in his heart. You understand he holds your heart as well. Jesus empowers you to hold the hearts of all who desire to understand and live from the wellspring of the Father's benevolence. You hold the hearts of those you love and those who have asked for your prayers. You give thanks for this experience.

FUTURE

From the heart of Jesus: John 13: 1-15

"Do you understand what I just did for you?"

Reflection: Jesus needed his disciples to understand his actions, as well as his words. He needed the disciples to recognize the importance of caring for all the needs or concerns a person may have so that those concerns do not occupy the space that otherwise could be used to experience Oneness. In washing the disciples' feet, Jesus prepared them in a physical sense for the journey that awaited them. He tried to remove their fears. He tried to dispel the angry words lodged at them for their association with him. From a spiritual perspective, by holding their feet in his hands, he attempted to propel them into the future—a future energized by the power that flowed from his hands. The touch of his hands would lead them to others. The apostles would bring his touch, his blessing wherever they walked.

Foot-washing can be seen as the ultimate act of forgiveness, a humbling act of service. By forgiving, one can release enough energy to embrace the present and live in freedom. By serving, one can identify and operate from the heart where there is no fear. Jesus needed his apostles to feel forgiven, to embrace all they would encounter and to live without fear.

Invitation: You are invited to enter your Sacred Space. In that space you find yourself waiting with the apostles for Jesus to come and wash your feet. You watch as he makes his way through the group. You wonder what each of them is thinking as the water is poured over their feet. You hear an objection. You watch Jesus smile as he counters the objection with words and water. Jesus stands before you. He does not say a word. You already have begun to release preconceived notions of what this experience would be like. You focus solely on the look in Jesus' eyes as the water flows from the pitcher.

You connect with Jesus' heart and realize all that limited you is being washed away by this water. You feel released from broken promises, unrealized dreams, shortcomings and insecurities. You feel open to this moment, open to the future and ready to undertake whatever you are called to do. This is a moment of grace. It is a moment of promise—the promise of a future of service to others. You understand that Jesus is sharing so much of himself with you in this moment. You understand that he is liberating you to be your true self.

Jesus invites you to pour the waters of forgiveness over your unrealized dreams. He knows that as much as you desire to let them go, they remain rooted inside you. He invites you to remove the fear that prohibited you from living those dreams. Tears flow from your heart and your dreams are given new life. Jesus shows you the way to realize your dreams now and in the future. Jesus shows you the way by his life.

You walk into the future knowing nothing can hold you back. You walk into the future without fear. You bless this moment and give thanks.

CATALYST

From the heart of Jesus: John 18: 1-19, 42

"Who is it you want? 'Jesus the Nazorean,' they replied. 'I am he;' he answered."

Reflection: It was no secret that those in power wanted to eliminate Jesus' influence over the people. So when the soldiers sought Jesus, he identified himself. Jesus was the Nazorean they were in search of, but he also was so much more. He was the Nazorean in relation to his heavenly Father. He was the Nazorean in relation to his followers, his family and his friends.

It was important for Jesus to know who he was, where he came from and what he meant to others. He was a man like each of them, but also the personification of oneness, wholeness, and harmony with his heavenly Father. He was hope. He was the catalyst for liberation. Even in his moment of crisis, Jesus did not believe he could be confined or contained by the words and actions of others.

Invitation: You are invited to enter your Sacred Space. You recognize the space as the Garden of Gethsemane. You remember the numerous times you heard this story of Jesus' experience in the Garden and already know the outcome of the encounter.

Jesus gives himself up without a fight even though he knows what is ahead of him. Jesus surrenders himself so as not to bring harm to his followers. He walks peacefully with those who have come to arrest him. He walks peacefully knowing who he truly is, knowing he will be the catalyst for liberation.

You watch the interaction between Jesus and the guards. Jesus knows who he is and is not intimidated by their taunts and rough handling. Jesus wishes they too could know who they truly are in that moment. Jesus wishes that he could share oneness, wholeness and harmony with them. He realizes that they are not ready to experience any of what he had to offer. Jesus realizes they are not yet ready for liberation.

You are moved by Jesus' presence of mind and serenity of heart. You find yourself asking how Jesus was able to be so peaceful under such dire circumstances. Suddenly the questions stop. Your mind is calm and your heart filled with peace. You realize that Jesus is silently asking you to join him in instilling calm and peace into this situation. You realize Jesus is asking you not to add to the chaos by your fear for his safety. You realize Jesus is asking you to help defuse the situation. He asks you to offer love to the hearts and minds of his captors and to captors of all times. Jesus is asking you to bring about change through love. He asks you to bring about liberation through love. You find yourself surrounding all captors with the Light of Love in hope that they treat all held captive with less vengeance, less violence. You realize that Jesus was captured not only for himself, but for all who were, or ever will be, held captive. You realize that Jesus allowed himself to be taken so that all people held unjustly could identify with him in their moments of captivity and realize true freedom and liberation in him. You realize Jesus the captive, becomes Jesus the Liberator, for all time. You bless this moment and give thanks.

LOVE

From the heart of Jesus: Mark 16: 1-7

"Who will roll back the stone for us from the entrance to the tomb?"

Reflection: While walking in the darkness the women realized that the stone placed to seal the tomb was larger than they could handle. They kept walking. They would not let the stone's size or weight stand in the way of ministering to Jesus. They would find a way to anoint the body of Jesus. They would not be stopped. The ritual would be completed, not out of obligation or duty, but because of love.

The women believed Jesus' message and lived from that belief system—needs would be answered, problems would be resolved and people experiencing sickness would be restored to a state of health. They knew in their hearts, the stone would be moved and they would be able to fulfill the required anointing. Nothing would be impossible for them because they embraced the energy of Jesus' words. They understood how Jesus' grace and energy would make all things possible.

Invitation: You are invited to enter your Sacred Space. You have removed the numerous stones in your life that have held your heart captive and you find yourself outside the tomb with the women waiting for the moment when you would see Jesus.

To everyone's surprise, the stone is no longer in the way. The tomb is empty. There is no sign of death, no sign of hopelessness. There is only an empty space and a feeling, a sensation that leads you and the others to believe something great has happened.

In your heart you sense that Jesus has already moved on. You sense that he has gone in search of all of you. You sense that he needed to see each of you, as much as all of you needed to see him. You sense he needed to make certain all those he loved survived the horror of the last few days.

In silence you begin the journey back to Galilee with the other women. Your mind and heart anticipate the encounter with Jesus. You wonder what he will be like. You wonder what you will feel when you see him once again. Your heart begins to prepare for the encounter. All the terror, the images that have taken hold of your waking hours, begin to dissolve. In your heart of hearts you know nothing will haunt you any longer. You will see Jesus. Of this you are truly certain. You will see Jesus.

The anger you harbored for those who killed him has been replaced with mercy, forgiveness unlike any experience you have ever known. You begin to wonder if this is what Jesus was trying to explain all along. You wonder if this was what his death really was all about. Your mind is on overdrive, yet your heart realizes only one thing matters—you will see Jesus again.

You bless all the people and situations in your life that wait for some transformation. You carry them in your heart as you walk toward your encounter with Jesus. You want them to experience Jesus as much as you do. You want them to know his grace, peace and mercy. You walk toward Jesus for your sake and for the benefit of others.

You walk in the name of those who are unable to walk and give thanks for this gift.

VIBRATIONS

From the heart of Jesus: John 20: 1-9

"Early in the morning on the first day of the week, while it was still dark, Mary Magdalene came to the tomb."

Reflection: It's no surprise that Mary Magdalene came to the tomb alone in the early hours of the morning. She cared deeply about Jesus and needed to be with him.

Questions haunted her. Who would continue his message? Who would offer her the liberation that she experienced with him, because of him? Magdalene came in search of answers, in search of an encounter. She came to make sense of the horrors of the previous hours. She sought harmony and oneness with Jesus. She expected to connect with Jesus on some level, on any level. His message, deep within her being, stirred feelings of expectation, rather than desperation. His message lived so vibrantly within her that she was incapable of anything but hope.

Invitation: You are invited to enter your Sacred Space. In that space you see Mary Magdalene in the distance. She is approaching the tomb with a sense of calm, a sense of peace. She comes to complete the traditional burial ritual by anointing the broken body of Jesus. You wonder why she isn't afraid to enter the enclosure alone. You wonder how many times has she anointed or assisted in anointing loved ones who have died. You wonder if those times prepared her for this moment. You wonder if any experience she ever had could have prepared her for this moment.

She stands before the space that contained the body of Jesus and realizes the stone is gone. She looks inside and is drawn to the place that once held Jesus. She continues to look, but does not understand. She can not comprehend the emptiness of the tomb.

"How could this be?" She continues to wonder," how could this be?

You find yourself standing with Mary outside the empty tomb. Memories of encounters with Jesus begin to gently well up in her mind and she begins to speak of them with you. You feel Jesus' presence from the past as he touched Mary and called her into new life. You feel Jesus' presence now as he breathes new life. You feel Jesus as he moved past the confines of death and into a new realm of being. You realize that Jesus' first breath of new life is the first breath of new life for all of creation. You find yourself breathing deeply of the same air that Jesus breathed. You find yourself seeing with new eyes, moving with a sense of expectancy and anticipation for all that is new, all that is good. You dwell on all that is to come.

Silence and stillness beckon you and Mary to sit on a nearby boulder. The air that Jesus breathed surrounds you. The sun that greets life in the morning with its brilliant rays begins to warm you. You realize this is a special moment. You bask in this holy moment, knowing this feeling is what first drew Mary to the tomb. You feel the vibrations of Jesus and draw strength from those vibrations. You feel oneness with Jesus. You remain in the silence in the stillness. You bless the moment. You open your heart to absorb more of the experience and you give thanks.

RENEWAL

From the heart of Jesus: Mt. 28: 8-15

"Suddenly, without warning, Jesus stood before them and said, 'Peace!'"

Reflection: Jesus began to make his presence known and felt through post-resurrection visits. To his followers filled with fear, he appeared with a greeting of peace. For their anxiety, he manifested a sense of calm, an energy that reinforced their experience of oneness with him.

Jesus desired to restore their sense of belief in harmony, in connection. He could do so only by embracing their shattered lives with his life, with his love. He could renew them only by his presence, either physically in their midst, or as a thought in their minds. Jesus knew the value of entering into his followers' hearts to lead them out of their feelings of hopelessness, into the sacred place of identification with him and the heavenly Father.

Jesus moves toward his disciples. They still are fearful. They don't understand. Jesus makes his way among them and offers a greeting of peace. They feel his presence and recognize his peacefulness. They find themselves growing less afraid. They begin to speak to one another confirming that each felt the presence of Jesus in his/her unique way. They find comfort in his presence.

Invitation: You are invited to enter your Sacred Space. In that space you find yourself waiting for Jesus. You know that he will meet you there. You feel empowered, energized from all previous encounters in this space with Jesus. You feel renewed and refreshed. Jesus' resurrection has been good for you. It has freed you from your fears. It has released all anxiety. It has restored balance in your life. You feel peaceful as you wait for Jesus. You acknowledge that you are waiting for Jesus' presence, but somehow you know he is already within you.

The room begins to fill with people. They too know they will find Jesus in this sacred space. They seem happy to be here. Burdens that once were too heavy to bear have been resolved. They seem ready to share Resurrection-joy, Resurrection-love with any one in need. They desire to share this new sense of life with everyone.

Jesus appears in the midst of the group. He does not need to speak. He does not need to touch. All recognize him and feel a profound connection to him. They do not need his words. They do not need his touch. They are one with him. They feel renewed, not only as individuals, but also as a group.

Jesus acknowledges that his resurrection was not for his sake only. He shares that in his resurrection, all have been resurrected. He shares that in embracing every moment that led to his death, he created a way of harmonization for all people. They no longer needed to fight, to reject any and all concerns. They would be asked to follow his example and embrace every experience. They would find themselves refreshed and renewed each moment of every day. A sense of peace and calm prevails throughout the room. You bless the experience and give thanks.

PURE JOY

From the heart of Jesus: John 20: 11-18

"Jesus said to her, 'Mary!' She turned to him and said, 'Rabbouni'."

Reflection: Jesus encountered Mary who left the house in darkness in search of him. Initially when she came in contact with him, she didn't recognize him. She thought he was the gardener tending to the area outside of the tomb. As Jesus called her name, he spoke to every fiber of her being. He spoke to all the places within her that at one time were in need of healing, in need of wholeness. He spoke to the person he had always known her to be.

Mary was in tune with his vibrations. Mary knew his voice. Without hesitation she recognized him. She cried out in response with her life, her hope, her longing, her joy—she cried out to him with all of herself.

He was alive within her. She could hear his voice. He was alive within her. She could feel the connection to him. The person she sought, she had become. The person she reached out for was already present within her being. Jesus was alive in every aspect of her being. She was totally alive because of that realization.

Invitation: You are invited to enter your Sacred Space. In that space you are outside the tomb looking for Jesus. You see others in the area doing the same. Each turns his/her head as if being called by someone. You hear your name and recognize the voice of Jesus. Yes, Jesus is calling your name. He is calling you to share in his resurrection experience. The joy of resurrection surrounds you. The joy of resurrection fills you. You feel complete by the resurrection of Jesus. You feel complete in and through the resurrection of Jesus.

You realize resurrection is not the end. You begin to see that resurrection is only the beginning. It is the beginning of seeing with new eyes, understanding with a heightened sense of awareness and feeling as if there is no separation between you and all people, no separation between you and all of creation.

You are graced with the knowledge that resurrection is connection. You are graced with the realization that resurrection is celebration, activity, presence and compassion. You realize that instead of fighting for those in need, you are called to invite them to stand up and claim what is rightfully theirs—resurrected life in and through Jesus' resurrection.

You realize that resurrection compels you to call others by name, as Jesus called you by name. Call them by name. Call them into new life.

Resurrection compels you to wake all who suffer from the slumber of disease, poverty, conflict, lack, oppression and confusion. Call them by name. Wake them into new life.

Resurrection-joy permeates your being. Give thanks and bless this step into new life.

REALIZATION

From the heart of Jesus: Luke 24: 13-35

"Stay with us. It is nearly evening—the day is practically over."

Reflection: Jesus accepted the role of the stranger for the couple on their journey to Emmaus. He walked with, listened to, and questioned them as they made their way home. As the couple grew more accustomed to his presence, they pressed him to remain with them. They feared for his safety and didn't want him to travel alone in the dark. The couple also felt there was something familiar about him. They knew they needed to spend more time together if they were to remember from where they knew him. The couple needed more of his words. They needed to feel the energy that flowed from him. They needed to share a meal in order to return to the space where he had taken them so often in the past.

The way he held the bread and cradled the cup of wine—they knew who he was. They knew this was Jesus. Tears of recognition streamed down their faces. This was the man they had grown so fond of. This was the man who spoke of liberation for all. As they embraced him, they realized what liberation truly was. As they embraced him they felt so in tune with him. The man and woman accepted the bread and wine from the hands of Jesus. It was food and drink from their home, but somehow he had made it his own. He had made it part of his very self. They accepted the bread and wine as a gift. They reflected on all they had seen and felt in the last few moments. They knew he will ask them to nourish others by this experience of liberation. He continued to speak to their hearts.

Invitation: Your Sacred Space awaits you. The food of realization, the food of recognition has been prepared. You sit with the couple in their Emmaus home. You watch as Jesus begins to share the bread and wine.

Jesus' hands take the bread and you realize that Jesus and the bread are one. There is no separation. As he passes the bread to you, you realize he is giving all that he is. He has identified with bread— bread that has sustained people for generations past and will feed generations to come. He desires to be the bread that brings Life for all. You accept the bread from his hands. You realize in that moment you are being invited to sustain people by your life.

Jesus' hands embrace the cup of wine. As he gazes into the cup you realize that he recognizes himself in the fruit of the vine that has brought healing to the sick, lifted spirits of the oppressed and quenched the thirsts of so many. Jesus identifies with the wine. He feels poured out. He feels that he too is a life giver, life sustainer and life liberator. You accept the cup of wine realizing no less is expected of your life.

You drink deeply from the cup knowing your life will be poured out for others as well. You bless the experience and give thanks.

REASSURANCE

From the heart of Jesus: Luke 24: 35-48

"Look at my hands and feet; it is really I. Touch me."

Reflection: Jesus needed to reassure his followers that he was still with them, he had not abandoned them. To one who thought he had seen a ghost or heard a memory call his name, Jesus offered his hands and feet. He encouraged his followers to touch him. Jesus needed to impress this encounter upon their memories.

"Touch me" Jesus said, implying do not be afraid—I will not hurt you. I come to you in love. I still care deeply about you. The horrors are past. They haven't changed my love for you. They haven't changed our relationship. Touch me, feel life—feel my energy move within you. Touch me—it is really me, the one you followed, the one you needed to believe in. Touch me—the one who brought you to this moment of realization that freedom, liberation, oneness, harmony and wholeness still belong to you. All that I have shared with you did not die with my death. All that I have promised you rose with new splendor the morning of my resurrection.

Invitation: Your Sacred Space is filled with the disciples. You see Thomas make his way across the room toward the others. He sees their excitement and wonders what has transformed their once heavy hearts. Jesus moves toward Thomas, and Thomas stops suddenly. Thomas appears confused. He appears unable to move. You realize the experience must be too much for him to comprehend. You know he was the one who needed proof, needed to really experience that Jesus had risen from the dead in order to believe that the words of the disciples were true and not wishful thinking.

Jesus understands Thomas' hesitancy. He knows that when Thomas is ready to believe, he will believe. He knows when Thomas is capable of moving into the space of the resurrection Thomas will greet him.

Jesus waits for Thomas to grow accustomed to him. Jesus waits. He does not speak. Jesus floods Thomas with his mercy. Jesus fills Thomas with his love. Jesus knows Thomas has felt the depth of his love and mercy. He sees it in his eyes and feels it in the softening of his stance. Thomas has experienced Jesus and has lived. Thomas has felt the grace of resurrection. Thomas moves into the space of Jesus. The others gather around him as he closes his eyes and is filled with resurrection-peace.

You feel that same peace. You feel the resurrected Jesus in your midst. He comes to you with gentleness. He comes to bring calm. You have been awakened to a new dimension for your benefit and the benefit of others. You want to experience this state of consciousness fully and simply open yourself to be flooded by resurrection-grace.

Your spirit expands. It soars to the heavens. Your heart opens as if drawn out by the notes of a song. The resurrected Jesus is present to all in the room, yet each feels his presence in his/her own way. The resurrected Jesus is present for all in the room fully, completely surrounded by resurrection-light. Bless this experience and give thanks.

FAMILIARITY

From the heart of Jesus: John 21: 1-14

"'Come and eat your meal,' Jesus told them. Not one of the disciples presumed to inquire, 'Who are you?' for they knew it was the Lord."

Reflection: Jesus appeared under ordinary circumstances, in familiar surroundings where the disciples were. He encouraged his disciples to come and eat, an act they had shared so often in the past. He was also calling them to partake of an experience that went beyond the physical act of nourishment.

They didn't need to question who he was. His actions, his attentiveness to their needs were enough for them. They knew this was Jesus, their Jesus. They heard his voice. They recognized his energy. They were embraced by his love and caring. Jesus made his presence felt to feed their bodies and to sustain their spirits. Jesus needed to be present in order to move them into the future.

Invitation: You enter your Sacred Space. You recognize the place as the site of the lakeside meal of Jesus and the disciples. The fire is burning. Jesus is preparing the meal and the disciples are hauling their boats to shore. You sense the disciples' happiness at being able to experience Jesus for a third time. You sense Jesus' desire to make his presence felt in a deeper way.

Food is shared. Words are spoken. You sense an expansion of space and time. No one is rushing back to the village to sell the fish. All simply relax in the comfort of the presence of Jesus. You relax in Jesus' presence as well. You sense you are being taught to take time and to savor special moments like this. You feel a special connection to Jesus at this moment.

Jesus encourages you to be open to whatever may come, to whatever you may find your self called to do. Jesus reminds you that you can recreate this moment of connection, comfort and presence whenever you remember him. He indicates that you can create this sacred space for others by simply calling his name or thinking of him.

You decide to call others into the presence of Jesus. You invite them to sit and experience the calm, the peace, the caring of Jesus. They sit in the sacred space open to all that Jesus has to offer. They accept the words, the gestures. They accept all that Jesus is and calls them to be.

The sacred space is a shore of safety. The winds and raging waters of confusion lose their ability to impact the lives of those who have chosen to seek shelter, refuge in the peace of Jesus on the shore. The ravages of hunger are replaced by the nourishment of Jesus, the living bread. All in need flock to Jesus. All in need find comfort on the shore. Jesus reaches out to all who place themselves before him. He feeds them with a word, a touch and asks you to do the same. You feed them with love and caring. You bless them as you have been blessed. You bless this experience and give thanks.

INVITATION

From the heart of Jesus: Mark 16: 9-15

"Go into the whole world and proclaim the good news to all creation."

Reflection: Jesus challenged the disciples to proclaim the good news—all they had seen and heard while with him: the blind see, the deaf hear, the lame walk, the dead rise up, those emotionally torn find peace, sinfulness is forgiven, abundance replaces lack, and those lost are now forever with the ones who love them.

The disciples' challenge becomes our challenge. Each of us is invited to live from the heart level where oneness is the norm. We are invited to expect abundance, joy, harmony, peace, healing and to share those expectations with people in need. We are invited to help people see beyond their limitations. We are invited to proclaim that our journey of healing led us to new places, sacred spaces where we experienced ourselves and others renewed, refreshed, restored, and connected to Jesus in a deeper way.

This is our good news—news so powerful it can't be contained or bottled up within. This is our good news—news that needs to be shared by all who traveled this healing journey together.

Invitation: The Sacred Space is filled with people surrounding Jesus. He is overjoyed by the size of the crowd. He is listening to the wonderful stories they recount of the healings that have occurred, the changes that have taken place in their lives and the lives of people near and dear to them. He encourages them to share the good news. He encourages them to continue to look for opportunities to inject peace, calm, wholeness and harmony into situations of need.

The crowd begins to disperse and Jesus motions for you to draw closer to him. He asks you to share all that you have experienced. He desires to hear what has changed in your life and the lives of others that you have carried with you into the sacred space. You seem hesitant to speak. You seem reluctant to share the good news.

Jesus understands. He was never one to look back either. He only moved forward to the next situation, the next person who was in need. But Jesus desires that you acknowledge all the good that has transpired over this journey of healing. He asks that you look deep inside and proclaim the good news. Jesus feels that good news and grace should be spoken about in order to offer hope to those in need. You begin to share with Jesus all that has happened during this journey.

Jesus listens. You recount situations, but also have questions. Jesus is happy to enter the space of your questions and surround you with peace and calm. You realize Jesus' true gift is his ability to diffuse false assumptions and negativity. You realize Jesus' gift is one that helps you to see situations and people through the eyes and the heart of the Father. This gift transforms all situations and elevates them to their original state of wholeness, harmony and oneness. With Jesus your heart is transformed. You begin to see all through the eyes of the Father and give thanks.

Jesus' Strength Becomes Our Strength

Jesus, in his struggles on the way to the cross, seems to embrace questions, not only with his mind, but also with his heart. He enters into a level of conflict that even those closest to him, do not appear to understand. The conflict is intense—it deals with Jesus being true to himself, regardless of the cost. His cries for freedom, for healing, for wholeness are uttered, but not heard. Those he expects to be supportive, slip away out of fear. They are not ready to be exposed, to be identified with Jesus. They are not ready to experience death because of their association with him. So Jesus walks with his own questions. He walks alone like so many on the road to healing.

Immerse yourself into the heart and mind of Jesus. Find yourself identifying with Jesus in the multitude of experiences he endures. Feel his merging with each situation every step along the way. Hear his cries. Feel his pain. Watch Jesus grow in strength of conviction as everything is taken from him. Watch those closest to Jesus surrender only to receive more than they could have imagined. Look closely as Jesus experiences transition into splendor.

Be with Jesus in spirit. Feel the New Life of resurrection. Smell the fresh spring grass. Hear the soft morning song of the birds. Listen for his footsteps as he moves toward your heart—to touch, to heal, to provide strength, to make you whole.

Enter Jesus' space. Embrace his silence. Be one with Jesus. Walk to the cross and into the promise of Resurrection.

Chapter 11—Healing Is Living The Questions

I. JESUS AND PILATE

I stand here, Father, silent.
Pilate paces back and forth.
Even he does not know what
to do with me!

Somewhere
in his heart, he knows that
death is not the answer,
but had no other choice
than to sentence me
to silence the crowds.

Father, why?
What have I done?

What was so wrong with
the way I preached?

What was so wrong with
the way I touched people's hearts?

What was so wrong with
the way I healed?

What made the crowds
so uncomfortable with me?

I don't know, Father.

All this is beyond me...

I never thought it
would be this way.
But You knew, Father,
didn't You?

So Father, here I am.

I am numb.

What else is there
for me to do?

If this is Your will,
I join myself to it.

If that will means death,
take me now, Father—
before I run away.

Take me now, Father—
before I grow too scared.

Father, I am standing here.
It's not Pilate, it is You I see.

I stand before You silent
and ready to begin
my walk of death.

II. JESUS AND THE WOOD

Father, this wood reminds me
of all the people You've
asked me to carry.
Their pain brings
tears to my eyes.

I see their stories
etched in this wood —
Stories engrained in
each worn line —

A widow's loneliness,

A brother's untimely death,

A mother-in-law's fever.

Father, tell me why
You've asked me to carry
all these people.
Just tell me why.

I've cared for and carried
so many time
and time again.
Where are they now?

Where are all the people
You've asked me to care for?
Where are all the people
you asked me to carry?

Have they run away scared?
So tell me, Father,
how this caring
will change things?

How will this carrying
of the cross make life
any different?

Father, don't get me wrong.
It's just that I am so numb
and this new pain adds
to my confusion.

Father, I need a "why"
before I can embrace the wood.

I need a "why" before
I can allow myself
to be further torn apart.

I need a "why" Father.
Don't you understand that?

The soldiers have gone.
It's only You and me, Father.
The "why"…

I need a "why"…

You ask.

You offer me the wood.

I am One with You, Father.

I see Your hands.

They are mine.

They are splintered.

I see the "why" —

You can no longer carry
the people alone.

I see the "why" in
Your heartblood,
in Your palmblood.

In my heart —

on my hands —

I see the "why".

Father, I take the wood
to myself.

I hold it tightly.

I take the wood to carry
Your people's pain,
my people's pain.

I embrace the wood.

I embrace the pain
knowing it has come
from You, Father —
knowing it is One with You.

Father, did I ever
have a choice?

To be myself—

Did I ever have
a choice, Father?

III. JESUS' FIRST FALL

Father, these people
are watching me.
They wait to see if I get up.
They wait to see if I can bring
myself to my feet and resume
this walk to my death.

It's so easy to remain here
and not deal with the questions
that fill my mind.

It's so easy to lay still and
forget the pain that awaits me.

The soldier's words are
watering my heart and mind.
They taunt the garden of madness
within me.

Father, I am down.

I don't know if I can get up.

I don't know even if getting up
would make a difference...

These questions, Father.

WILL I BE ABLE TO ENDURE?

WILL I SCREAM OUT?

WILL I CRY OUT?

WILL I BE THE SON
YOU ASK ME TO BE?

Feelings of insecurity,
fear, doubt.

I am not comfortable with
these feelings...
They are new to me.

These feelings are expressions
of a self I don't know, a self
I have never experienced.

Father, take the questions from me.
I just don't know.

Tap the spring of Your strength
within me.

Urge me to stand up
to begin again.

Chapter 12—Healing Is Living While Letting Go

IV. JESUS AND HIS MOTHER

I never meant to put her through this.
I never meant for her to see me this way.
Yet she stands here, Father, and she walks
each step of this journey with me.

She can't speak, Father.
Her body has become one with my pain.

Her only son, her life,
her dream is slipping away
right before her eyes.

Father, does she have to experience
all this pain? Couldn't she have
been spared? Father, why?

Why do You call her to endure this pain?

Father, I look into her eyes.

Her heart is torn.

She wants to change places
with me, yet she knows she can't.

Tell me, Father, why did it have
to come to this?

She taught me everything I know.

She taught me all that is
of any importance.

She even spoke to me of You.

She spoke of life.

She carried me through
Joseph's death. Who will carry
her now as she watches me die?

Father, why do you ask her
to become one with my pain?

Why, Father?

She is my mother—
such a beautiful person,
a totally giving woman.

Yet You call her to suffer.

And she has no choice—
mothers always carry
their children's pain.

Father, why?

You love her, yet
You still call her
to embrace my pain.

She accepts it in the same way
she has accepted all the pain
You've ever asked her to bear.

And there has been so much pain—

When she thought I was lost in the temple—

The times I was on the road for days—

The days after Joseph's death—

And the time of my insecurity at Cana.

Father, she has been through so much...

Now this—this Calvary Walk
and Golgotha to come.

She will stand by and take it all in with
the same eyes that once watched
me grow into who I am today.

I love her, Father, but it's
just so difficult to release
the feeling of not wanting her
to bear my pain.
But You ask me
to release this feeling.
You ask me at this second
to release all.

So take all, Father.

Take it from me.

Fill her emptiness.

Share her suffering.

Love her through the pain.

V. JESUS AND SIMON

Father, it's so difficult to accept
the help of others when I am so
accustomed to being the one who helps.
It's so hard to accept the fact that
I need to be carried, instead of
being the one who carries.

I am so confused.

You've always called me
to carry others, even in
my darkest moments, and now
I am so weak from all the questions
that I can't go on without
someone walking by my side.

Father, this is all so new —
so strange to me.

I'm so accustomed to being alone —

alone at prayer with You
in the mountains, by the water,
and even in the middle of a field
filled with hungry people.

I'm accustomed to being alone,
yet not alone because I know
You were always there with me
even if I didn't experience
Your presence.

But now, Father, You ask me
to accept the help of this man, Simon.

You ask me to stop and allow
another to shoulder some of
this weighted wood.

I can see now that You are slowly
changing my perspective of carrying.

Father, You teach me
so many things—
Are You now trying to teach me
that to be able to carry
I must be open to being carried?

Must I know what it means
to be carried so as to carry
others more deeply,
to hold them with my heart?

Father, I accept Simon's help.
Simon, and all the other Simons
that may enter my life to be
grace for the moment.

I am grateful for all You
have taught me through him.

I am grateful You called him
to be the one who carried me.
It could have been so different if
You had chosen someone else.

But You called this Cyrenian.
He asked no questions—
he only reached out and became one
with this piece of wood.

He touched my heart.
He opened my mind.
He showed me what carrying
and being carried is all about.

VI. JESUS AND VERONICA

I saw her eyes, Father
long before I felt her hands.

I knew she would try to
break through the crowd
and touch me, somehow.

I could feel it, Father.
I could feel it.

I wanted to stop her—
spare her what could be
unnecessary pain, but she kept
walking, pushing through the
crowd of confused people.

She touched me and stirred
feelings I had never felt before.

She didn't have to, Father,
or did she? She could have
gotten lost in the crowd...
But she chose to step out
and touch me with hands that
spoke of tenderness and love.

Father, I was afraid for her.

I was afraid the soldiers
would try to stop her and
hurt her if she refused
to be stopped.
But somehow,
she slipped through, and

reached me long before
they could block her path.

Father, her hands felt
so good, so gentle
as they touched my face.

Her hands brought healing.
They eased my pain
as only a woman's hands
are able to do.

Her hands were a gift
to me in my moment
of pain.

Why did You
choose to gift me with
that sign of grace?

What was I supposed to
learn in that holy moment?

Father, I was always
the one who touched.

I was always the one
who brought comfort
to the people
with my hands.

This is all so new,

so overwhelming...

I accept Veronica's hands, Father.

I open myself to the healing
they hold for me.

I welcome the tenderness
in her eyes, the gentle reminder
of Your support in her voice.

Father, I thank You for this
special sign—Your sign of oneness
with me, Your reminder that I am
not alone.

Thank you, Father for sending me proof
of Your presence in my suffering, through
the gift of Veronica's hands.

Chapter 13—Healing Is Living In Alignment

VII. JESUS' SECOND FALL

Father, suppose You give me
more time? Veronica has just made
Your presence felt to me in spite of
all the pain. What about the others?

What about the women, men, and
children who line this road?
Maybe all they need is more
time also to feel Your presence
in their midst?

Father, wouldn't my life mean more
to them than my death? Why should
my death affect them more than my life?

Please tell me, Father.
Tell me if You can...

Look at their faces, Father.

After I die, what will their lives be like?
Will life be the same for them as before?

If yes, then it all seems so ridiculous,
so lifeless, so worthless.

People wandering in search of hope,
in search of joy, a sense of connection.

More time, Father. Just give me more time.

Maybe then, with different words—

with moments of caring I will be
able to be a sign of Your presence
among them...

Maybe I can open
their ears, their hearts in a new way?

Maybe I have changed in this moment
and can reach out to them in a way
they will be better able to understand?

Father, this fall is worse than
the first fall. These questions
tear me apart.

I feel I can give
so much more. I know I can be
more present. I am not ready
to die.

Do You hear me?

Do You understand?

I am not ready to die.

These questions challenge me.

They break my heart.

They drown my spirit.

I've fallen with them
and with the many faces
that look to me for
signs of hope.

I have no answers that
would lift me out of myself.

Accept these questions, Father.

Accept all that you call me to do
for the people who line my path.

You've given me these people.

They are Your own.

Reach out through Simon.

Raise me up from my desire
to affect their lives.

Let me see with Your eyes.

I don't seek answers.
The questions are loud enough
at this time.

Accept me
as I am, Father.

Raise me up.

Help me to walk on.

VIII. JESUS AND A WOMAN'S TEARS

Look at them all, Father.
The Women and the Children of Jerusalem.
Look at their tears—they align themselves
with my suffering. Their hearts split in two
as they identify with my struggle.

They see me bruised. They see me beaten.

They recognize their brokenness in my being.

There is one woman with deep,
brown eyes—look, Father...

Her tears flow from her heart.

They have been bathed by her spirit.

They spring from her deepest needs
and move her into a state of oneness
with me in my moment of need.

I look into her eyes.
They are eyes who have
sought me out before.

I cry in pain with her.

I cry for her. I cry for me.

I am consumed by her love.

Oh, Father, this woman has touched me before.

She has anointed me with her perfume.

She has bathed my feet with her tears.

This woman, Father,

this Woman of Perfume and Tears

has made my death walk possible

for a few more steps.

My spirit joins her spirit
as we both are being beaten
by emotions too powerful to contain.

Father, her tears have softened me.
They are grace in this chaotic moment.

I give her my tears.

I give her my heart.

The pain of unknowing
has made us one in You.

IX. JESUS' THIRD FALL

Father, I am back on the ground.
I've fallen once again.
Time, proximity to death brings on
this question: "Where do I go from here?"

Father, each time I've stumbled
and fallen, You've taken me back.
My falls have made no difference to You.
You continue to embrace me with Your love.

This fall is different, Father.
I don't know where to go from here.
I know death awaits me,
but really don't know what death means.

We've walked and rewalked
too many steps in this journey.
I've seen sides of me I never
knew were there.

But You knew, Father.

You knew in order to
realize who I am, I had to
endure rejection,
abandonment,
uncertainty —
Golgotha to come.

Father, no more questions.

The pain is so unbearable that
it has to be just You and me now.

In silence... Just You and me.

Still my heart.
Quiet my mind.
Give strength to my legs.

In silence, I move
one more step into You.

Chapter 14—Healing Is Living In Realization

X. JESUS IS STRIPPED

Father, I stand here
on this hill for all to see.

The soldiers strip me
of the tunic my mother
had woven for me.

They strip me of something
so precious, despite its bloodiness.

This tunic was my last connection
with the one who gave me life.

Father, I stand here exposed.

My family and friends stand with me.
They wait. They scream inside.

They beg, they plead for my life.
We all know I will die.

They've come this far with me,
hoping for some intervention,
some sign from You.

Father, help me.

In this moment of vulnerability,
may I realize who I am.

May my family and friends
come to know who I am.

So, Father, I ask You to help me
embrace this moment.

I know Your strength is within me,
but need to feel that strength now.

Prepare me for my death.
It is only seconds away.

Ready my heart. Prepare my
whole being as I go into You.

XI. JESUS' ANGUISH

The soldiers have finally asked
for this beam of wood.
They snatch it from my hands.
I let go as the wood burns my skin.
I let go, knowing I am that much
closer to death.

Father, I surrender myself.
I put myself in their hands.
They throw me down.
My body hurts in ways it
has never hurt before.

I thought once I let go
You would take the pain
from me, Father.
I thought once I let go, You
would give all back to me.

The pain has gotten worse.
It blinds me. I flinch and try
to draw my ankles and wrists away
only to experience more intense pain.

Father, take this pain. I give it
back to You. I have no options,
no choice. There is nothing
more for me to do.

No words, no gestures.
Only love.

I embrace the pain.
Only love.

The pain is unbearable.

I embrace the moment.
I look for my mother.
She embraces me
with her eyes.

I feel Your love
through her eyes.

XII. JESUS' FINAL MOMENT

Father, all the past moments
of letting go have prepared me
for this final moment.
I face death and I am
no longer afraid.

The pain of this steel,
these nails, this wood
rubbing against my body
grips me, but not nearly
as much as the pain I feel
when I look down and see
my Mother, John, Magdalene,
and a few other friends.

Their hearts scream in anguish.
I feel so sorry for them.
Father that is why I know
the time has come.
I must embrace death.
I must become one with death.

I can't ask them to suffer any longer.
I can't ask them to bear more pain.

They've come this far and are drained.
They've shared every step
of this journey with me.

Father, I put my life into Your hands.
I give back everything that is/was me.

Father, You've given me all—
I know that. I am one with You, Father.
I am One with You.

Father, take me.

Take my spirit.

Rejoin it to Your Spirit.

Let it become Spirit.

Father, in this darkness
I know Oneness with You.

I feel as if we had never been apart,
as if there had never been the
fragmented questions of hours ago,
days ago, years ago.

It has taken me this long to realize
my Oneness with You.

Into Your hands, Father.

Into Your hands I place my spirit.

I give it back to You because my spirit
is Your Spirit.

I return what is Yours
back to You.

XIII. A MOTHER'S ANGUISH

What am I supposed to say?
What am I supposed to think?
What am I supposed to feel
at this moment?

My son...

Your son...

I hold his body
in my arms.

The One You had given to me—
to love, to raise, to cherish
on this earth...

My son...

Your son...

His friends take him down
from the wood that held him.
They slide him into my arms
to hold one last time.

My son...

Your son...

I embrace him
and give him back to You
all in the same breath.

Questions plague my mind—

Could I have spared him this pain?

Could I have changed things for him?

Deep within me Your Silence—

Deep within me Your Emptiness—
You called him to this life.

He embraced the call.

To live any other way,
he would not have been true
to himself.

I am his mother.
He is Your Son.

In the silence of his heart,
he has seen You.

He knows You and
all Your ways.

I hold him close to my heart.

I am his mother.
I will always be his mother.

My son... Your son...

Chapter 15—Healing Is Living For Others

XIV. FRIENDS OF JESUS

Father, You gave us Jesus.
Now You call him back to You.
We let go of this man
who has touched us so deeply.
He was gift to us and for us—
only now have we begun to see that.

He taught us to move through difficult
moments by living life without fear.

He joined himself to moments
of uncertainty, of vulnerability,
of weakness and all was transformed
in his embrace.

Nothing was his, yet all was his.

No one was his, yet all were his
in the moving through,
in embracing all that
required letting go.

We lay him in this tomb now.

We give him back to You.

Where will You take him?

Where will his spirit go?

We place Jesus near the earth.

We lift his spirit up to You.

We give him back to You
with our tears, with brokenness
in our hearts.

Will You ever give him
back to us again?

XV. NEW LIFE

What's this I feel?
Is this life, Father?
You've called me from
one life to ONE-LIFE.
You've whispered my name.
You've touched my heart.
You've sung life/ONE-LIFE
INTO ME.

You've strummed a
Resurrection Song
on the strings of my heart.
You've breathed Oneness
throughout my being.
I can not contain the love
I feel, the love I AM.
It draws me from this tomb
onto the fresh morning grass.
It draws me from
NOTHINGNESS INTO
EVERYTHINGNESS.

Father, this is LIFE:
healing the sick,
feeding the hungry,
providing shelter and clothing
to those in need,
touching with LOVE
all those who've yet
to experience LOVE.

You call me LIFE, Father.
You call me LOVE.
You call me to embody LOVE—
the LOVE that is You, Father,
the LOVE that is me.
The LOVE THAT IS.

The sun calls.
The birds sing waiting
for me to run from this tomb
out onto morning's fresh stillness.
They wait to hear that NEW LIFE
has come from the pain, through
the process, in the embracing of all
that has been asked of me.

I must run, Father!
I must run and see Mary.
I must run and see my mother,
John, Peter, James, Andrew,
and above all, Thomas!

They must see.
They must touch.
They must feel this
new side of LIFE/LOVE.
Perhaps then they will
begin to understand?
Perhaps they will dare enough
to dream of what could be
when lives are lived in
ONENESS with You, Father.

I have to tell them!
And then I have to show them—
They must see.
They must touch.
They must feel this
ONENESS with You.

XVI. GENTLE THOUGHTS

So it has come to this, Father:
my family, a few close friends,
and me on this mountain.
The sun shines on our shoulders.
The wind tosses our hair.
Spring flowers line the path
that leads me back to You.

So Father, I lift myself up,
no longer crossed on a beam,
but alive, and moving closer
in each thought to You.
The gentle image of You
stirs within me.
It compels me to
close my eyes and
leave all behind.

I close my eyes
and find myself at home
within myself.

HOME—ONENESS with You
even though I am still here
on this mountain.

I am here, yet not here.

I am One in a way
I had known Oneness
a long time ago.

Printed in the United States
201732BV00002B/1-156/P